THE HEART OF THE GOSPEL

THE HEART OF THE GOSPEL

BY THE REV.
J. K. MOZLEY, D.D.
LECTURER OF LEEDS PARISH CHURCH, AND PRINCIPAL OF THE
CLERGY SCHOOL
EXAMINING CHAPLAIN TO THE BISHOP OF RIPON

WITH A PREFACE BY
THOMAS B. STRONG, D.D.
BISHOP OF OXFORD

WIPF & STOCK · Eugene, Oregon

Wipf and Stock Publishers
199 W 8th Ave, Suite 3
Eugene, OR 97401

The Heart of the Gospel
By Mozley, J. K. and Strong, Thomas B.
Softcover ISBN-13: 978-1-6667-3442-3
Hardcover ISBN-13: 978-1-6667-9025-2
eBook ISBN-13: 978-1-6667-9026-9
Publication date 8/24/2021
Previously published by SPCK, 1925

This edition is a scanned facsimile of
the original edition published in 1925.

TO
PETER TAYLOR FORSYTH
IN GRATEFUL AND AFFECTIONATE REMEMBRANCE
AND TO
GEOFFREY ANKETELL STUDDERT-KENNEDY
IN CONTINUING FRIENDSHIP
PREACHERS IN DIVERS PORTIONS AND IN DIVERS MANNERS
OF THE CROSS OF CHRIST

PREFACE

THE doctrine of the Atonement held a large and almost exclusive position in the theology of the Reformers. A recovery of the sense of individual salvation was one of the strongest motive forces of the Reformation. Down to the early days of the nineteenth century this doctrine formed the main subject of the sermons of a large number of English Churchmen and of more Nonconformists. The Tractarians shifted the attention of Churchmen to the fourth and fifth centuries, and to the problems connected with the Incarnation and the Church. Also, the Liberal school of thinkers tended to move away from the special field connected with the Atonement. The doctrine of vicarious sacrifice presented difficulties to persons who began to think in terms of the new theory of evolution. We may say, therefore, that the doctrine of the Atonement, though never disappearing from English theology, lost some of its former prominence during this period.

Mr. Mozley's book reminds us that it is still the Heart of the Gospel. He does not deny or smooth over any of the difficulties which modern minds find in it; still less does he water down or attenuate its meaning. But he writes of it in the light of the recent drift of theology; he discusses the questions that have been raised about it in modern books; and, what is of primary importance, he presents it in connexion with the whole view of the Nature of God and His relation to man and the course of the world's history. Mr. Mozley is no novice in the studies connected with this doctrine, and I am sure that those into whose hands this book may fall will find the doctrine itself set out clear of incumbrances and of the difficulties which may be brought against it from various sides of modern thought. I commend the book most cordially to the attention of the Church.

THOMAS RIPON.

December 23, 1924.

INTRODUCTION

THE volume to which this is an introduction is made up of addresses, articles, and reviews composed within the limits of almost exactly five years. Despite the independent character of most of them, so far as origin is concerned, it is my hope that they will be found to present a common view of the meaning of the Christian Gospel, and to suggest a unity in approach and treatment. If that is in any way the case, it will be because of the essential unity of the three words, Gospel, Bible, Doctrine, which form, as it were, the foundation of the thoughts to which expression is given in this book. Something much more elaborate would be needed in order to make clear the character, both ideal and real, of the relations existing between Biblical and Dogmatic Theology and the dependence of both upon the Gospel which gives to each its grounding. But, as something much less than a formal treatise along these lines, this volume may, perhaps, direct attention towards the need for a positive theology which is always in close touch with the Bible and makes a wider appeal than to the intellect alone. Especially do I feel the need that the greatness of the New Testament revelation of the Person and the Work of Christ should illuminate the theological presentations of Christianity. It would be foolish to underestimate the seriousness of the issues which confront us in connexion with the doctrine of the Church, of the Ministry and of the Sacraments. Yet it is possible to lay such emphasis on these great matters as to be in danger of a certain lack of proportion. We are safest when our whole thought and devotion is steeped in the spirit of the most triumphant question which we inherit from Apostolic Christianity—" He that spared not His own Son, but delivered Him up for us all, how shall He not also with Him freely give us all things ? "

Of the component parts of the book, " The Atonement (i) " was an address at Manchester Cathedral in February 1922, reprinted from *Fundamentals of the Faith* by the courtesy of Mr. F. B. Palmer. " The Atonement (ii) " was given at the Leicester Church Congress of 1919, and " The Atonement (iii) " at the Scottish Church Congress of 1924. " The Meaning of Calvary " was a paper read before the Anglo-Catholic Congress in London in July 1923. It is reprinted from the Report of that Congress by leave of the Congress Committee and the Society of SS. Peter and Paul, to both of which bodies I wish to express my thanks. " The Theology of Dr. Forsyth " appeared in *The Expositor* of February and March 1922, and I am indebted to Messrs. Hodder & Stoughton for their kind permission to make this further use of it. The next two sections are reprinted from the October and November numbers of *Theology* in 1920. " The Person of our Lord " was the subject of a paper read at the Leeds Anglo-Catholic Congress in June 1922, and appeared in *Theology* in September 1922, and " The Gospel and the Person of our Lord " of a paper at the Sheffield Church Congress of 1922. The final section,

INTRODUCTION

entitled "The Holy Spirit in the Church," was, in the first instance, given at the Manchester Anglo-Catholic Congress in October 1922.

Here and there I have made certain changes from the original form, but the substance of the work remains essentially unaltered, and, in particular, I have kept the personal note which belongs to papers which were addresses to Congress meetings.

In connexion with the construction of the book, I wish to express my indebtedness and gratitude to Miss Maud Bousfield, formerly secretary of the Anglican Fellowship, who kindly read through a mass of material and made most useful suggestions as to selection; and also to the Rev. W. K. Lowther Clarke for his interest and advice. Nor can I pass over in silence the great kindness of the Bishop of Ripon in writing a preface to this volume. For that act of his, with its generous gift of his time, and for whatever measure of approval he can give to what I have said, I am most grateful.

J. K. M.

LEEDS,
11th Dec., 1924.

CONTENTS

		PAGE
I.	THE ATONEMENT (i)	9
	THE ATONEMENT (ii)	34
	THE ATONEMENT (iii)	44
II.	THE MEANING OF CALVARY	56
III.	THE THEOLOGY OF DR. FORSYTH	66
IV.	THE WORK OF CHRIST IN MODERN THEOLOGY	110
V.	DR. RASHDALL ON THE ATONEMENT	128
VI.	THE PERSON OF OUR LORD	150
VII.	THE GOSPEL AND THE PERSON OF OUR LORD	164
VIII.	THE HOLY SPIRIT IN THE CHURCH	177

THE HEART OF THE GOSPEL

I

THE ATONEMENT

(1)

THE Bible is a library of books, but it is much more than that. It is a unity controlled by one faith and looking forward to the accomplishment of one purpose. The faith is belief in God, the purpose which is to be fulfilled is the establishment of God's Kingdom in accordance with God's Will, and not only its establishment but its perpetuity. Thus the faith in God which distinguishes the Bible as one book from every other book is also, to this extent, faith in man and in the world, that the world is the sphere within which, and man the instrument through which, God's purposes can be wrought out. The horizons of the Bible do indeed pass beyond the world and beyond man. As the revelation which is in the Bible moves forward with gathering weight and wider sweep, the horizons lift and let us through to a vision both of the world and of man in which their present conditions and values are seen as but the potencies of a future, transcendent glory. But the change is not from either a world or men, essentially bad, to a new creation in which the old is lost. There is no radical pessimism in the Bible. The world is God's world, and man is made in the image of God. There is no such contrast between eternity and time as would make the things of time and the men of time of small account. The world and its life is not a shadow but a sacrament. Within the life of the world works the eternal life, and man in his changing estate can ever rest upon the changelessness of God. He hath set eternity within their hearts.

But the Bible never allows us to think of the changelessness of God as though that stood in any opposition to the truth of His action. Such an opposition has not been unknown in philosophy, but it is foreign to the Bible. In the Bible, God is always in action. And His action is essentially moral action, directed towards good ends, whose realization would mean the achievement, by degrees, of those purposes which constitute, when taken all together, the one end which God has set before Himself. The Bible brings out for us what sometimes seems to be forgotten in an age so greatly concerned with man, and ready at times to put man in the centre and make God the great accessory to man's designs, that the final end of all existence is the end which God has set before Himself. The Bible lets us see what God is by showing us what God does. When we read there of qualities or attributes of God, those attributes are viewed actively in relation to God's fulfilment of His purposes. We do not possess in the Bible a formal list of them. We know them as they are manifested in action towards the world and towards men. So it is with God's anger and sorrow, His justice and mercy, His holiness and His love. There is no reason at all for

THE ATONEMENT

being troubled, because the Bible ascribes to God the feelings and passions of men. A God of Whom we could not think in this way would be a God useless to man. He would not react upon the world in any way that man could understand. If we could not think of God as possessing and manifesting the feelings which, in our case, accompany moral action, we could not understand His moral action. But as it is we know Him because we are known by Him. And His knowledge of us and of all the world is a knowledge which can no more be separated from feeling than it can be separated from will. He knows us as those called to the service of His Kingdom, that is to the doing of His Will. He has called us, not coldly, but in love. To attribute to Him indifference of feeling at any point which concerns the correspondence of man's action in the world with God's purposes for the world and for man, which are part of God's great and final self-end, is to do Him no honour. Where we have God in action, there we have the dynamic of His holy love.

Let us go a step further. The Bible is a book far more realistic than speculative. It has, of course, its profoundly mysterious side. But its mysteries are never simply transcendent. They are within the world as well as above it. They are related to the world's life as it is. They are to be spiritually discerned, but through moral insight rather than mystic trance or rhapsody. They are not like the mysteries of Theosophy. That is nowhere clearer than in the Bible's treatment of evil. It is busy with the problem not of its existence, but of its cure. It is interested neither in explaining it nor in explaining it away. Especially is it concerned with evil in its opposition to God. Evil is an energy acting against God's purposes. But it is an energy not latent in the nature of things, but set to work by the action of wills which possess a measure of that freedom which God possesses in its fullness. How it is possible for such freedom to exist the Bible does not inquire; but it assumes the fact. And the evil which consists in this energy of action directed away from God's ends, that is from His Kingdom, is what the Bible means by sin. Neither with regard to God's Kingdom, nor with regard to sin, is one uniform view presented in the Bible. We are conscious of lower and higher forms, and of the fact of progress. But it is along those lines that the problem of life is construed. Reality, if we may import the word, is basally and centrally moral. The world's crisis lies in the contest for the maintenance and victory of all that allies itself with the will of God over the positive evil which assails both that will and its servants. And it is further characteristic of the Bible that its view of evil, or, to speak more formally, its doctrine of sin, does not conceive of evil as no more than a succession of evil acts. There is a unity about evil which is the counterpart, even if the caricature, of the unity of good, and when theologians have spoken of a kingdom of evil they have been true to the spirit of the Bible. Evil is organic, with its roots deep in the past. Of that account must be taken in the cure of evil, which is also the vindication of God's purposes in the face of evil, and, in its most intimate meaning for God Himself in His personal relation to the world, so far as we are at all able to think of so great a matter, the justification of God.

It is against this background that the Atonement stands out. The Biblical view of atonement is intelligible only when taken along with the Biblical view of God and the world. If that view is rejected, if a less close connexion is made between the moral and the religious, if the world presents itself as a puzzle to be pieced together, rather than as a drama working through tragedy to reconciliation by whatever means are drastic enough to draw the sting of the one and to create not only the possibility but the fact of the other, it is not to be expected that the Atonement should be appreciated. Again, if the world's life is seen, indeed, as full of moral meaning, yet with the closely locked forces of good and evil so evenly balanced that there can be no assurance of the issue, there will be no place for any preaching of the certainty of atonement. For these two things go together—atonement, and the certainty that victory lies with the good. To believe in the Atonement is to have the security of that grandest optimism which rises from no buoyancy of temperament, but is born into the soul which knows that it can move freely in a world redeemed to its furthest corner and in its inmost heart by a God Whose love never fails, nor is His arm shortened that it cannot save.

I

There is a passage in the Sermon on the Mount in which our Lord says that He came not to destroy but to fulfil. Though He does not actually say to fulfil "the Law and the Prophets," and though we may think of His work as fulfilment in the widest sense, the primary reference is obviously to the Jewish dispensation on its legal and prophetic sides. Christian belief in the Atonement as the work of Christ becomes more luminous when account is taken of the Old Testament treatment of sin. On the one hand, there are the prophets with their intense moral earnestness, proclaiming the need for repentance and amendment. On the other, the law enshrining a sacrificial system with, as its object, the restoration of those right relationships with God which have been forfeited by sin. Neither Law nor Prophets give us the whole of what is needful. The earlier prophets react sharply against the sacrificial system when that is made a substitute for morality, though one cannot say that they disapproved of the principle of sacrifice for sin in itself, or were heedless of the disabling power and pressure of a guilty conscience which does not face the future because it cannot face the past. The vision which led to Isaiah's call brought with it a consciousness of guilt which had to be purged away before he could be sent on his mission. But it is in the Law that this side of Hebrew religion is developed. There the need for a settlement with the past is clear enough. The danger lies in formalism and in an assessment of ceremonial offences as on a level with the moral. Moreover, for the graver moral sins no atonement was possible. But just as in the Prophets God stands behind the individual and puts His words into His messenger's mouth, so in the Law the sacrificial system is not interpreted as being just man's self-chosen means of securing once again God's alienated favour. Here, too, God is beforehand with man. God gives to the people the blood upon the altar that they may make atonement for their souls. That the Law and the Prophets did not stand for two irreconcilable aspects of religion is shown by the work of Ezekiel, while the union of the profoundest degree of prophetic inspiration with the principle of atonement through vicarious suffering is manifest in the fifty-third chapter of Isaiah. And it should be noted that in that chapter the suffering servant of the Lord does not simply suffer because others have sinned: he suffers because he stands in their place and is able, in virtue of his innocence, to bear the burden both of their sins and of the penalties that follow. The innocence of the sufferer did not create a problem for the writer of this chapter, perhaps the greatest in the whole of the Old Testament; it was the outstanding fact which enabled a problem to be solved, or rather, a need to be met, namely, the restoration of sinners to fellowship with God. It would be pedantry of the most earthbound order to arraign the righteousness of God as it is revealed in this chapter; few Christians would think otherwise, or that a defence of the picture given is a serious and difficult ethical need. And yet many of the objections which have been raised against whatever type of atonement-doctrine speaks of Christ as standing in our place, bearing man's sin and submitting to sin's penalty, do, in logic, break like the waves of a hostile sea against it. Its æsthetic impressiveness cannot justify it if it is morally distorted

But the witness it has always borne to itself is to its moral greatness, and there, if anywhere in the Old Testament, heart speaks to heart.

An older theology than ours used to speak of the three offices of Christ, of how Christ came as at once Prophet, Priest, and King. We may have forgotten the phraseology, but the thought remains sound. The prophetic line revived in John the Baptist; and in Jesus too, at the very outset of His Galilean ministry, the prophetic strain is clearly heard. But His ministry is not the ministry of one who confined himself within the ranks of the prophets. A prophet belongs to a class; Messiah is unique; and that Jesus accepted the belief, and made Himself the claim that He was the Messiah, can be doubted only when an attitude towards the Gospel, altogether more suspicious than scientific, develops into extreme scepticism. Nor is it adequate to say that Jesus believed that He was Messiah-designate and would return to earth, clothed with full Messianic royalty. The verdict of the Gospels is that He claimed to be Messiah before His death, and there is no satisfactory reason for setting this verdict aside. If we would present the Messianic idea in a modern equivalent we might say that Jesus thought of Himself as King of the world. But in what sense, through what means, was He priest? How did He become our great High Priest Who has passed through the heavens?

The textual evidence, if taken by itself, is of small extent, though very powerful in quality and not at all easy to shake. There are the words in which He spoke of giving His life a ransom for many; there are

THE ATONEMENT

the words and the action at the Last Supper, when He broke the bread and said, "This is My Body," and took a cup and said, "This is My Blood of the covenant which is shed for many." But the belief that our Lord ascribed to His death a real efficacy, or saving value on behalf of men, does not need to base itself only on this narrow, if strong, foundation. Unless His death possessed in anticipation a significance which made it the crisis of His ministry, as climax and not as debacle, the end of that ministry is unintelligible. He went gravely and persistently forward to a death which He foresaw. That is the record of the Gospels, and there is nothing to set against it except the objection that if He had told the disciples that He was going to die, their failure to understand Him, and their surprise at the event itself, are incomprehensible. But this is an objection which fails to take adequate account of the fact that the violent death of the Messiah was not a conception for which they would be able to find any place in the general apparatus of their thought. But what did His death mean to Him? It meant this, at least, the Will of God. He did not go to Jerusalem haphazard, or simply hoping for the best and prepared for the worst. He went to Jerusalem to die there. Apart from this intention, which the Gospels show us so clearly to have been His, the whole of the life of Jesus, from Peter's confession at Cæsarea Philippi onwards, is not only an unreadable riddle, but one which ends in a purposeless catastrophe. But if He went to Jerusalem to die there, with His knowledge that He was the Messiah and of His consequent unique relationship to the

Kingdom of God, it could only be because His death was an integral factor in the purposes of God.

And so the Apostolic Church interpreted it. Early was it realized that the death was no accident, but something that had been prepared for in the deep counsels of God. We cannot trace the onward course of reflection upon the significance of the death of God's Messiah, but we know that St. Paul, for all that he did in the enrichment of its theology, was not the inventor of a new doctrine. What he preached that he received, that Christ died for our sins according to the Scriptures. The mass effect in the New Testament of this utterance of Christian faith is immense. Whatever uncertainties in respect of the dogmatic convictions of the early Church confront us in the New Testament, there is no uncertainty here. There is not one settled, uniform theology, there is not one, and only one, type of conception utilized for the interpretation of Christ's death. But there is an absolutely radical connexion between the religious blessings which man has from God and the Blood of Christ. There is a note of high exaltation which penetrates passage after passage, in which the thought is of what Christ has done for men through His death on the Cross, which testifies to the inability of the Church to contemplate that great theme without bursting forth into praise. That great line of Bishop Heber's Eucharistic hymn, "And in Whose death our sins are dead," has about it the very ring of the New Testament Gospel. What we have in the New Testament is creative or rather re-creative redemption. And it is no redemption easily achieved, no fruit of a

THE ATONEMENT

divine "Fiat," as creation is portrayed in Genesis. But redemption was a work that cost God dear, and it is in relation to that fact and idea that we rise to a theology of atonement.

It is at this point that many modern difficulties begin. It is one thing to admit, indeed gladly to acknowledge, that Christianity is a religion of redemption, that with the reality of liberation from sin is bound up the particular character of Christianity, and that this liberation has some sort of connexion with the death of Christ. It is another to confess that redemption from sin is through atonement for sin, and that He Who bears our sins does so not merely by taking them away from us through the arousing within us of a new power, but by taking them upon Himself, so that we have no longer the oppression of guilt-consciousness and of a moral account with God still unsettled.

II

Let us leave the difficulty, and, with it, what still remains to be said about the New Testament, over for the moment, until we have learnt whatever a brief conspectus of the workings of the Christian mind as revealed in historical development is able to teach us. There are six movements, which do not present the picture of a formal succession of stages, but are often seen overlapping and interpenetrating, yet discernible and divisible as rotating on different centres of religious emphasis, that demand notice. First, there is the explanation of the death of Christ, the earliest, outside the New Testament, which can be called in any sense a formal theory, that Christ redeemed men by paying a ransom to the devil, who possessed some sort of right, not always clearly defined, over the souls of men because of human sin. In exchange for the captive souls of men the devil grasped at the human soul of Christ. But that soul had never sinned; the devil had no right to it and could not retain it. He had overreached himself, and thereby lost whatever rights he had possessed over men. This is a piece of dialectic, to us quite strange and even grotesque, based on the supposed need for discovering someone to whom Christ gave His life, or His soul, as a ransom for many, and on the assumption that that person could only be the devil. Yet it gave expression to the very profound early Christian conviction that every power of evil was overcome by Christ in His Cross, that there He had broken down the tyranny of Satan.

Secondly, we may note the belief, which was specially characteristic of some of the great theologians of the Christian East, that the Incarnation was itself in a real measure redemptive, since the Son of God when He became man did by that act introduce a new and purifying element into human nature. The union of the divine and the human in Christ was potent for all humanity, and humanity was conceived of quasi-physically as a substance in which a new leaven was working. This idea reappears in somewhat altered form in the modern notion of Christ as the Representative Man, Who, because He is not just one individual among the millions of individual men that go to make up the human race, but a Person essentially divine,

THE ATONEMENT

Who, in the words of the Christmas Collect, has taken our nature upon Him, can so act on behalf of men that what He does by the perfection of His obedience, which reaches its climax in the Cross, they can be regarded as doing in Him. The strength of this line of thought consists in its attempt to show that whatever Christ does for man He does not do externally to man; but that as mankind as a unity has sinned, so mankind as a unity makes amends for sin in Christ, its perfect representative. Its weaknesses are that the conception of what is sometimes called " Christ's inclusive humanity " is a difficult one for us to assimilate, that to lay the stress of interpretation on what man does in Christ rather than on what Christ does for man is, on the whole, to move away from the religious centre of the New Testament, and that the theory is not self-sufficient: it needs to be helped out from other sources before we can say what it is that Christ, or mankind in Christ, does to make amends for sin.

In the third place stands the doctrine which goes back to one of the greatest of our Archbishops of Canterbury, St. Anselm. He taught that man by his sin has done the gravest of injuries to the honour of God, and that for that wrong satisfaction must be given. But this is beyond man's powers; so the Son of God became man that He might do for man, and as man, what man cannot do for himself. This He did by His death, which He, the sinless one, did not need to undergo. With this supreme sacrifice God the Father was well pleased, and as the Son had nothing to ask for Himself, He asked for and received for His brethren, the men who should believe on Him, the remission of the eternal penalty which was due to their sins. Anselm's *Cur Deus Homo?*—Why did God become man?—is the most famous single book on the Atonement which has ever been written. Its inadequacies have often been pointed out; its view of sin as an offence against God's honour is mediæval in form and remote from our standpoint; it is in danger of making a sharp and unreal distinction between justice and mercy in God, and of associating, in an impossible way, the Father with the principle of justice, the Son with the principle of mercy; and with regard to the relationship of the death of Christ to the forgiveness of sins, it is not at all a satisfying account of the matter to say that as Christ, in virtue of His sinlessness, did not need to die, God was bound in justice to reward this free act of sacrifice, and that the reward is transferred to men. On the other hand, it is reasonable to subordinate all these important defects of the theory to its one great merit, that it teaches that sin makes a real difference to God, so that God's purposes cannot be worked out until the moral situation which results from sin has been transformed.

We pass, fourthly, to the view which is still, I imagine, often regarded as the orthodox doctrine of the Atonement: that sin must be punished, and that Christ, the divine and sinless Person, bore the punishment of sin in the place of men, becoming their substitute in His death. The substance of this view, regarded as a theoretical interpretation of the New Testament, is far older than the sixteenth century,

THE ATONEMENT

but it was in the sixteenth century, and especially in Continental Protestantism, that this doctrine of what is often called penal substitution was given definitive expression. It is against this view of the Atonement more than any other that there has been a widespread reaction. And undoubtedly, as it has been presented by theologians and proclaimed by evangelists and preachers, it has given ground for very various opposition. It has weighed sin and punishment almost as though they were two articles which must exactly balance; it has construed the relationship between Christ and men in too external a manner, and has not avoided the impression of a mechanical and non-ethical shifting of the punishment due to men on to Christ, and of the perfect righteousness of Christ back to men; above all, it has not been free from the danger of subordinating the love of God to His retributive justice, with the result that love seems to be a contingent attribute of God, justice a necessary one. And as in the previous theory, a ditheistic severance between the Father and the Son in the work of man's salvation has lurked too near, though in the background. Modern theologians, who stand within the tradition of this view more than of any other, have not been insensible of these grave perils, and have set themselves to the task of moralizing the theory without abandoning the values which it harbours. This is especially the case in the work of the late Dr. P. T. Forsyth. Those values are a deep sense of the inevitable tension and clash between sin and the holiness of God, a refusal to give up the ethical nexus between sin and punishment and judgment, and a conviction altogether greater than any mere *theorem* of the theological schools that Christ did for men in relation to God, and on the scale of the world's sin, something which man could not do for himself, and which did really and for ever change the moral situation as between God and man.

Fifthly, with interest concentrated on the thought that for the forgiveness of sin adequate repentance is necessary, and with the realization that such repentance is beyond human power, Christ has been viewed as the perfect penitent, Who, just because He was personally sinless, was able to express on behalf of the race with which He had identified Himself a penitence well-pleasing to the Father. This theory came into prominence through the remarkable writings in which, with considerable differences both of time and method between them, it was embodied, in Scotland by Dr. McLeod Campbell in *The Nature of the Atonement*, in England by Dr. R. C. Moberly in *Atonement and Personality*. But I cannot regard it as destined to any long life. When every explanation possible has been given, the difficulty of the idea of vicarious repentance in the case of one personally sinless is too stubborn to be overcome.

Finally, there is that presentation of the Atonement which emphasizes not any direct objective God-ward action of the death of Christ, but the influence of that death upon man through the revelation which it gives of the completeness of Christ's self-sacrificing love. His death was, indeed, necessary because His whole mission led inevitably to that climax, but it was not necessary in any sense of reparation or satisfaction to

THE ATONEMENT

God, of expiation of sin or bearing of sin's punishment. One of the acutest minds of the Middle Ages, Peter Abelard, gave early utterance to this " moral influence " theory, as it has been called, when he spoke of the Cross as the supreme exhibition of love which should enkindle a corresponding love in the hearts of men. It is a theory which has, within the last few years, been expounded in England in the learned and powerful Bampton Lectures of Dr. Rashdall. It frees itself from all the characteristic difficulties of other types of doctrine by denying the general presupposition of those types—namely, that the Passion of Christ has, primarily and effectually, a God-ward reference and meaning. But that freedom is purchased, as I cannot but hold, at far too high a price. Why that is so, and how far we can ally ourselves with any one presentation of the Atonement, will come before us in the final part of this paper, in which, with this brief historical statement before us, we shall try to serve ourselves of the deepest substance and Gospel of the New Testament.

III

A saying which has gained some considerable vogue runs somewhat as follows: "It is the fact of the Atonement which saves us, and not any particular theory." And this is true if it means that the greatness of what Christ has done has its way with us, though we cannot find satisfaction in any particular conception of the method, or even though we may hold to one which fuller knowledge or insight might bring us to reject as inadequate or misleading. Nevertheless, we do well to be suspicious of such an aphorism, for the Atonement can no more be a bare fact than a sacrament can be a mere sign. In the fact of the Atonement there is necessarily involved the faith that He is able by the greatness of His Person and the laying down of his life on the Cross so to work in adverse relation to our sins that a new and true religious and moral union with God opens out before us. It is necessary to underline successively and all together each word in the brief statement, "Christ died for our sins," and to allow that if this does not mean not by potential implication, but by positive condensation, that Christ by His death did something for the blessedness of sinners, it is difficult to see that it means anything at all. Interpretations of this fundamental meaning have, as we have seen, widely differed, but an original agreement, which carries with it a nucleus of dogmatic, unites all Christians as they see Christ crucified, in St. Paul's strong expression, *placarded* before them.

But I believe we can go rather further as to the measure of agreement. Granted that Christ's death is a fontal and creative fact, which blesses sinners by its powerful bearing upon their need of union with God, the effectual working of the fact is along the two lines of forgiveness and of freedom. These two lines are neither parallels nor one line sharply broken into at a point where forgiveness points backwards as the antidote neutralising all the accumulated evil of the past, and freedom points forward as the power capable of dealing with whatever reassertion of evil may threaten in the future. They are lines that without

THE ATONEMENT

being two by sharp distinction, or one through prolongation, are mutually necessary, interdependent in energy, testifying to a common source and prophetic of a common goal. The reconciliation of man with God, pointing forward to the union of man with God in the completeness of an eternal life, is realized in experience as forgiveness and freedom. And that these blessings in their characteristic Christian form are so surely linked with the Cross of Christ that the certainty of their reality which the Christian possesses is unintelligible apart from the Cross, is a conviction in which widely diverse doctrines of the death of Christ yet find themselves at one. All Christian experience enshrines at least this much of the appropriation of the saving paradox of that death.

The New Testament, however, as a whole, which enshrines the faith of the primitive Church and gives us the weight of apostolic testimony, compels us to go further. I say " as a whole," for it is not a matter in which we come to the truth by selections of texts. These have an evidential value as illustrations which exceeds in importance their relevance to a particular passage or argument. And that the New Testament outlook can be confined within the limits of any exclusive moral influence theory is a position far more irreconcilable with the facts than the attempts which have sometimes been made to find in the New Testament a fully established doctrine of objective atonement. The New Testament is preoccupied with God, and with Christ as God's representative rather than man's. The idea of mediation runs through it; the relations between God and man are not regarded as they conceivably might be in a world where God was at work for the salvation of men, but where there was no Person and no Cross of Christ. The teaching of Jesus bears witness to this, for it is impossible to show from the Gospels that in respect of the Kingdom of God He ever ranked Himself with men as simply one of those whose privilege it would be to receive and enter into the Kingdom. That the grace of God is at work among men through the presence in their midst of the Person of Jesus—nothing less than that is the Gospel which we find in the Synoptic Gospels, and it is the presupposition of the faith of the early Church raised to a higher level, which offered a wider and more penetrating vision through the Resurrection. The movement in the Gospels is double, from God to man in the Person of Jesus and from man back again to God through Jesus. And the nodal point is the Cross. In the Cross the principle of mediation reaches its highest sense; it transcends all its own previous past, which moved towards, and prepared for, the crisis but was not the crisis itself. Just as, regarded as historical tragedy, the life of Jesus culminates in His death, so, conceived as the channel of God's gracious dealings with men, it pours the full force of the stream which flows within it into the Cross. It is the grace of God overflowing in the death of Christ which evokes the magnificent response of adoring gratitude which opens to us, time and again, the heart of the Apostolic Church. It is not what Christ is doing in them, but what He had done for them, and not in anticipation or potency alone, which is the great and open secret of the New Testament. The atmosphere is completely different from anything we could conceive of its being had the primary interpretation of the Cross, much more the sole one, been of its power to stimulate men to repentance or love. Repentance and love have indeed discovered in the Cross that which draws out their utmost resources, but if either the direct aim or most far-reaching result of the Cross was to make men penitent or to awaken them to love, the New Testament is a misleading book, with its emphasis continually misplaced.

But it is one thing to contend for an objective attitude towards the death of Christ, as that of the New Testament writings, and another to argue that one precise construction is put upon the fact of His death. I certainly would not try to maintain the presence of one, and only one, dogmatic type. I should allow that St. Paul, the Epistle to the Hebrews, and the Johannine writings approach the idea of atonement with, in each case, special and particular interests uppermost. And this variety within the New Testament has its complement in the restraint of the great Creed of Christendom, which is content to affirm that the Lord Jesus Christ was crucified for us under Pontius Pilate. It may be asked whether in this case it is worth while trying to grasp the meaning of the Atonement in any more detailed way, whether any real religious interest constrains us to push our inquiries beyond a general assent to the certainty of God's gracious will having reached its redemptive zenith in the Cross, whether we do not plunge ourselves into insoluble dilemmas, which matter the more because of their moral and not merely intellectual density, if we try to probe further into a mystery that presents itself as the victorious counterpart and reversal of the mystery of evil. One may readily sympathize with such pleas, and still hold that the risk must be taken and the attempt made, that Christianity as at once a comprehensive philosophy of religion and a practical force, as a religion not departmentally, but through vital inter-association, sacramental, ethical and mystical, lacks its full stature and power of command so long as Christian thought about the Atonement refuses to venture beyond the limits of statements as to the general relationships of the Atonement.

Start with the reality of God's love. We are all agreed that the work of Christ is given to us out of the exceeding love of God and is not creative of it. That love that gave us the Incarnation gave us also the Cross. But love cannot be safely treated as no more than a feeling. It is not expansive benevolence, be the situation what it may. On the contrary, it must inevitably manifest itself as purposeful action dealing with every situation according to its final needs. Love is not the whole of moral reality, however much it may be the one power which is capable of re-creating moral reality after the true pattern. And love must pay the price which recreative action may entail. God on Calvary is the price of God at Pentecost. And love in conflict with sin can only draw the sting of sin by being willing to endure what sin draws down upon itself through the reaction from it of that holiness of God which, in relation to the world, stands for the preservation of the integrity of the moral order. That reaction at its most solemn and intense is what we call judgment. Sometimes the impression is given that love is regarded as a substitute for holiness and judgment, so that it is not necessary to trouble much about these latter if only we are sure of love. I can find no justification for this view, whether in the New Testament or in the deliverances of conscience, or in the richest Christian experience. God's holiness was not in abeyance when in Christ He was reconciling the world to Himself, nor His judgment upon sin suspended. The victory of the Cross lay in its consummation of Christ's lifelong confession of God's holiness through the perfect sacrificial offering of Himself by the undeviating energy of His Will to the service of God's Kingdom, and, *pari passu*, in the judgment there executed upon sin, a judgment final in kind, because the crisis of Christ's life was also the crisis of evil's effort for world-mastery. For evil to fail then and there was to fail irretrievably and for ever. And according as we look on the one hand on Christ's confession of God's holiness brought to perfection in the Cross, on the other on the judgment upon sin which went along with it, we shall see that there is something which we can by no means afford to give up in the old ideas of the satisfaction which He made to God, and of the penalty of sin which He took upon Himself. Get away from all feudal, commercial, transactional, quantitative forms of thought, as most truly we need to do, and a deepened moral and spiritual insight will learn how to make use of the belief that God makes the Cross of Christ at once the throne of judgment and the fountain of salvation. It is when we convert great words like sacrifice or expiation into a system of unspiritual mechanics that the harm is done, and the stumbling-block of a hard logical calculation bars the way to God ; but the remedy is not to dispense with them nor to eviscerate them of their challenging force, but to place them within a deeply moralized context of God's controversy with the world in all its ethical fullness. And behind that controversy is the fullness of the Life of God, perfect as only holy love can be perfect.

And then as to ourselves : how can we think of the Atonement so as to avoid a doctrine of external relationships ? It is through the faith which sees God bringing Himself in Christ into unity with us, so that from that unity may spring an answering unity of ours with Him. But we must not think of the unity as secured by the self-limitation of God through incarnation in our nature, which then raises human nature to the level of the Divine. The identification is complete, not in the Son of God made man, but in the Son of God made sin. The key to that boldest of all St. Paul's sayings is to be found in a vision of the cost to God of the hallowing of His Holy Name in a world where the power of evil is so great and subtle, and mankind as a unity bears in its history, so deeply scored with the tragic marks of its guilt, the proof of its great need. Over against that unity rises the higher unity of mankind in Christ, the unity of mankind redeemed because God in Christ has immersed Himself in all the evil of man's estate, and by a mystic act of moral self-identification taken upon

THE ATONEMENT

Himself the weight of sin and of the judgment which follows sin, the judgment of His own holiness, and opened a great door through which man can pass into the blessed experience of forgiveness and freedom and eternal life.

It is on the greatness of the crucified Christ that the Church lives. The treasuries of her devotion draw their richness from that distinctive and triumphant Gospel. Her greatest act of worship is steeped, as it always has been, in the adoration of the Lamb that was slain and has taken away the sins of the world. The symbolism of her greatest art in architecture and painting and music has been a tribute to the King who reigned from the tree :

> Thou, O Christ, art all I want,
> More than all in Thee I find—

that is the measure of her gratitude to Him Who summed up and surpassed every sacrifice in the sacrifice of Himself. The Church must unlearn her hymns of praise before she can unlearn her faith in atonement made, and not to make. She will never unlearn them. Never will come the time when she, from out of the fullness of a heart kept in peace, a peace which is the trophy and spoil of God's royal warfare and victory in the Cross of His Son Christ our Lord, will cease to make the confession of all that she owes to Him who has given her all :

> Mine is the sin, but Thine the righteousness,
>   Mine is the guilt, but Thine the cleansing blood,
> Here is my robe, my refuge and my peace,
>   Thy blood, Thy righteousness, O Lord my God.

THE ATONEMENT

(II)

AT the Cambridge Church Congress of 1910 a meeting was devoted to an examination of " The Apocalyptic Element in our Lord's Teaching: its significance for Christian Faith and Ethics." The subject reflected the interest which Schweitzer and the eschatological school of interpretation had aroused. And there was more than interest; there was unrest. For if that school were at all in the right there was need of a good deal of fresh thinking on the Gospels and on the presentation of Christian theology. Powerful influences had been at work to teach that the centre of the Christian message, as revealed in the synoptic narratives, was the proclamation of the fatherhood and love of God, and the manifestation of the Divine Kingdom in the gradual spiritual uprising and response of humanity. But what if the centre were really to be found in the thought of a sudden, heaven-sent catastrophe, of the Kingdom visibly established amid the ruins of a dissolving world, and, finally, of the unique death of the Herald of the Kingdom, Who, when it came, should come Himself as the Son of Man, and, because it tarried, gave His life to hasten its appearing ? If this, or anything like this, were true, Christian theology and Christian religion would have to take account of it. The popular view that the Gospel

THE ATONEMENT

sanctioned optimistic hopes of human progress and continuous spiritual development would need revision. An unsparingly radical treatment of the evangelical narratives was giving back the sense of profound mystery enfolding the very beginnings of the Gospel, a mystery to which but little justice was done in the reduction of the Gospel as preached by Christ to a simplicity more thin than massive.

The eschatologists were a school of critics. And critics often have a keener eye for faults in others, their misreading of a situation or omission of some vital factor, than in themselves. These critics were no exception; they had the keenest of eyes for the weaknesses of an opponent's position, but their own offered many an opportunity for attack, which was promptly seized. Nevertheless, there was real constructive value in the raising of the question which they had set themselves to answer—What was the character of the religious centre around which the Gospel, as originally proclaimed, had revolved? For since truth is a complex, nothing is more important to its appreciation than the discovery of where, among its several elements, the true emphasis is to be laid.

The eschatologists had challenged much popular religious thinking. The war exploded it. Beliefs which had rested largely on the assumption that the world's history would slowly broaden down from precedent to precedent, and that the assurance of an orderly moral progress was sealed in Christian faith, were shattered. The demand for theological restatement grew loud. It was evident that dark clouds hung over the secret of God's relationship to the world; there was no open vision. What was the secret? Did God not care? Or was His power far less than His love? To say Amen to this last was for many the best way out. A limited God, toiling up the Hill Difficulty with His creatures, seemed a tolerable and credible conception. To some of us it seemed to surrender what made God mean God to us; to make God in our own image may, in the long run, prove as much lacking in utility as it is a depreciation of truth.

It is well to see exactly what had happened. The war had not created the moral problem, though some spoke as though this were the case. But it had deepened it. It had thrown ethical questions into high relief, above all, the supreme ethical question, whether morality is the nature of things, and existence moves forwards towards a moral end. It had called upon the mighty moral ideas, those solemn names which though often forgotten had yet maintained their hold upon humanity, to descend from the heights, and show themselves as realities or shadows. Was there a final meaning and worth in righteousness established through sacrifice and passing into judgment? The highest moral justification of the war as a single though immense incident approached it along those lines. The sacrifice had been for the establishment of certain ends, and in the sacrifice love had been manifested as the servant of righteousness, spending itself for something grasped as infinitely precious truth. But the justification of the war was not enough; belief in a righteous cause is but one more instance of delusion if you cannot see the righteousness of the cause within the greater framework of a righteous world. There could

THE ATONEMENT

be no final justification of the war if there was not at the same time the justification of God.

The justification of God. It is good that we have been made to face so stupendous a necessity. It gets us away from a humanitarianism which will slip man into the centre of things, and sees the life of God clearly only when it is busy with the life of man. But if God exists He cannot find the end of His existence and action simply in what concerns man. He would be inferior to man had He not ends of His own to fulfil. The believers in a finite God have seen that; but I do not think that on their premises they can assure us that God will ever achieve those ends. But if God cannot achieve His ends, then there never can be a fully moralized universe, which recalls, but in a more serious form, Plato's view that God in creating makes the world as good as the character of the material upon which He works will allow.

The world then, in the light of the war, has revealed itself as a huge moral question, riddle and paradox. Men have asked for an explanation adequate to the appalling reality of the facts of moral and physical evil. Now Christians have from the first been familiar with that sense of moral paradox, of apparently unbearable catastrophe which opens on to salvation, of evil that goes so deep and yet less deep than the judgment which descends upon it, and than the grace which is its antidote. For at the centre of the Christian Gospel stands the Cross of Christ.

" To the Jews a stumbling-block and to the Greeks foolishness." How should it not be? To speak of salvation, and to find the Saviour there. What object was there in such a spectacle, what final end of God's will could it serve? And even when men have found Christ crucified to be the power and wisdom of God, the old wonder has remained, revealing itself in the continual search for some thread of doctrine that should conduct to the very heart of the mystery, to the great meaning hidden in the words, Who for us men and for our salvation came down . . . was incarnate . . . was crucified.

You cannot reach the inmost ethical soul of the Cross, any more than of the war, and find God justified in either, if you stop at heroic self-sacrifice. The greatest love needs an end worthy of the quality of its sacrifice. The Cross was the gift of God's love, it proved God's love; but it was not in order to prove God's love that Christ died upon the Cross. The death of the Son of God was not the supreme object-lesson to make manifest the love of the Father. But within the sphere of the mystery that encloses the opposition between good and evil, between the holiness of God and the sin of man, is to be found the cause why, in Christ's own words, His suffering and death are viewed as necessary. The Son of Man *must* suffer many things . . . and be killed. It is not true that the New Testament speaks with many unharmonious voices on the death of Christ. One thought recurs again and again: that death is God's answer to and settlement with sin; in Christ shedding His blood for the remission of sins, bearing sins, putting away sins, made sin, we are brought to that moral centre of things where the supreme righteousness of God is manifested, and God justifies Himself for ever. I say " for ever," because the Cross is not an episode, nor even a glorious victory in the campaign against evil, with goodness seen for a moment more than equal to the worst which evil can do against it ; but a final achievement. The Cross, if the New Testament view be taken, means that we do live in a world where the only permanent and triumphant values are the moral values, a world where righteousness is a reality, and judgment, and atonement, and reconciliation. Such a world is one that we can trust in respect of the one thing which ultimately matters, the end towards which it moves, because we know what is to be found at the end of it, namely, a holiness which has endured the full blast of evil directed against it, and has taken to itself the experience of the penalty which follows, though individuals may seem to escape it, in the tracks of sin, and a love which sets up salvation in the midst of judgment, so that the condemnation of sin shall not mean the destruction of the sinner.

The Gospel as we have received it brings God far more fully into the world, into far deeper contact with the world's evil, than any doctrine of a finite God can do. In that doctrine God's range is limited ; His moral aspirations are greater than—so it may be—His moral capacities ; even for Him, where final moral issues are concerned, His reach may be greater than His grasp. But in the Gospel God has in the Cross of Christ done that which leaves the moral issue settled, not by a mechanical expulsion of evil, through an act of sheer power, but by an act great enough and rich enough in its moral quality to meet every need which is bound up with the presence of evil in the world, every need which must be met if there is to be a real justification of God. Christianity is the religion of perfect morality, not because of the loftiness of its precepts—a loftiness however pre-eminent in degree, yet not unique in kind—but because away beyond the region of precepts, and of human obedience to them, it reveals a God Whose righteousness is declared in His own action, in the truly unique thing which He has done.

Let me return for a moment to that question of self-sacrifice. On the day I write there appears in *The Times* a letter from a distinguished Cambridge scholar, in the course of which he holds up as an ideal at which we need to aim the manifestation of self-sacrifice, whereby each man may appear " as Christ." But this falls far below the Christian valuation of Christ's work; it does not give us the whole Christ of the New Testament and of Christian experience. It may well provoke the retort, fatal to a sense of the true relationship in which we stand to Christ, which, as I have been told, was made by a man at the front: " Do not talk about Christ: we see Christ here every day." Undoubtedly so, in kind at any rate, if the measure of Christ's greatness is to be found in what He suffers on the Cross, rather than in what He does there. But it is not His passive obedience which makes Him our Lord and King. The atonement and redemption which we have in Him, which binds us to Him by a stronger tie than that which exists because He is our Creator, is the fruit of this activity, of His work done both for God and man in the Cross. Reconciliation is a hard enough thing to achieve between

THE ATONEMENT

men, a reconciliation which does not overlook and forget but settles with the evil burden of the past; but the reconciliation of the Cross is a far greater thing because it is the reconciliation of the world to God, with full account taken of the moral rift that opens between a holy God and a world involved in a common guilt. If the war has not taught us that we cannot separate the idea of reconciliation from that of atonement, that we are still far from the ethical centre of things if we keep love and expiation apart as though they had nothing to do with one another, we have been slow to mark the signs of our times. The place of satisfaction, reparation, atonement, in the re-establishment of moral relationships which have been shattered by sin is here, ready to be marked by the seeing eye and hearing ear. Those are no barren concepts, the mere conventional coinage of theologians, which ordinary folk can dispense with and ignore. Theologians have made use of them for the interpretation of the Cross in their attempt to understand what it was that Christ did there for God in the matter of evil; but they were in the world long before the day of Calvary, troubling men's consciences and stirring them to ask questions and give answers in which half-lights of truth, unconscious heralds of the revelation to be testified in due time, shed here and there illumination upon the puzzle of the world's good and evil and of God's attitude to it. Whatever else the Cross is in the theology of the Atonement, it is not an answer to an irrelevant and unimportant question.

In our generation the old questionings are once more heard, in greater volume, in greater intensity, than ever before. The war has made of the world something far more than an intellectual enigma—a moral challenge. After all, if the world in which we live is not a moral world, if goodness is not at the heart of it, living even in its devastating fires, then nothing finally matters; defiance of the world-order and acquiescence in it are all one in the end; conscience becomes the worst of deceivers because it creates for us the image of a world to which nothing, in reality, corresponds. Men cry for more light; and still it is true, *Via Crucis Via Lucis.* The mystery of the Cross is the illuminating mystery. The word of the Cross is the power of God, telling of what God has done in taking upon Himself in His only Son a burden too great for sinful man to carry, revealing what sin is, and the judgment which falls upon it, and the atonement which is made for it, revealing God as holy and gracious love, as the Father of His people Who forgives their sins, not sparing the cost to Himself of a forgiveness which left no moral claim—the vindication of His holiness and the penalty of sin—unprovided for. If we could only see even so awful a fact as the war against the background of what the death of Christ meant to God, of what was done when the Father gave the Son to be lifted up from the earth, we should know with a certainty that perhaps would make itself felt through all the inadequacy of words, that there can be no question of God not caring for man, no question of His power being less than what the world's evil needs. Our hearts and minds would catch that spark of religious conviction which burns up all doubt, as St. Paul cries: " He Who spared not His own Son, but delivered Him

THE ATONEMENT

up for us all, how shall He not also with Him also freely give us all things ? "

That is a Gospel equal to our times, for it is the Gospel of a world redeemed and secured in God, despite and through all the evil and sin which not yet are visibly put beneath the feet of the world's Redeemer. And in the Cross of our Lord, in all its strain and the agony which broke His heart, there is for us the peace of God's eternity, the life of God, which was poured our there that we might live.

THE ATONEMENT

(III)

It is evident from the New Testament that the new faith, or religion, or Gospel, in whatever terms it might be expressed, or whatever aspect or relationship of it was being expounded, could be regarded as a mystery. The word occurs first of all in our New Testament in connexion with the knowledge of the Kingdom of God which is given to the Lord's chosen disciples in contrast with the multitudes which can learn only through parables. In the Epistles of St. Paul it appears in a number of different contexts, but always, except for two passages in the Pastorals, with an involution of the ideas of secrecy and revelation. In Rom. xvi. 25 the mystery is God's purpose for the world now at last made known through the preaching of Jesus as the Messiah ; in 1 Cor. iv. 1 the mysteries of God are those secrets of the divine plan which the Christian minister is empowered to communicate to others ; in Ephesians, where the importance of the word provides one of the dominant motifs of the Epistle, it has special relation to God's universal purpose for humanity manifested by the inclusion of the Gentiles ; while in Col. i. 26, 27, this thought is enlarged by the identification of the mystery with the Person of Christ, "who is in you Gentiles." We need not go further into the usages of the word, which is found also in the Apocalypse ; but

THE ATONEMENT

a comparison of the various passages where it is introduced would fortify the conclusion which may be drawn from but a few that, if the primitive Church had a correct sense of the essential nature of the Gospel, then the element of mystery interpreted as God's illuminative revelation of His secret purposes is indispensable within Christianity. And where there is such revelation we are near to the thought of God's self-justification, of Theodicy.

But along with the recognition of this essential mystery-element in Christianity there should go a realization of the error of conceiving of the religion presented to us in the New Testament as but one special form of that contemporary religious impulse and orientation to which, as involving a cultus and a theology of a particular kind, the general title of " Mystery-Religion " has been given. The fact that it has been possible to give such very different accounts of New Testament Christianity is sufficient proof of that. For those accounts have gone wrong, not in finding something which is not there, but in emphasising some actual element in such a disproportionate manner as to throw both it and everything else out of focus. Primitive Christianity was compact of religious experience, of dogmatic theology, of eschatological expectation, of moral idealism, of a worship itself richly combining filial confidence and fraternal loyalty. It is the combination of these elements into a unity on the basis of certain historical occurrences, wherein the Church saw the signs of special divine action, which gives Christianity as we meet it in the New Testament its unique character. It is possible to allow that definite contributions were made to it from the Greek and the Oriental, as well as from the Hebraic side (though what has been suggested in this connection has often been very far from proved), and at the same time to maintain that our greater knowledge of the process of growth and development leaves the wonder of that vital religion, from which ours to-day derives, unaffected—the whole is far more than the assemblage of its parts.

So I should say that no tabulation of the parts, however accurately made, will explain the whole. Now let us start with the whole and pass from it to the parts or elements or forces which undoubtedly we can observe in it. We shall then confess that not all these elements are of equal value and universality. Not all are indispensable in the form in which we discover them in the New Testament. Such is the Parousia-hope, the expectation of our Lord's second coming at an early date. Such is the argument from prophecy as resting on a series of detailed correspondences between sayings and doings centuries apart. Such is that attitude towards grievous moral backsliding in Christians which, however the relevant passages be interpreted, has a grounding in the Epistle to the Hebrews and left its mark, even if by way of modification, in the Church's disciplinary measures. And while there is a New Testament theology, and it is right to protest vigorously against any treatment of the New Testament which reduces the importance of its theological side, we shall not reach it by an analysis of the theological statements in the Synoptic Gospels, then in St. Paul, then in St. Peter, and so on, till a

THE ATONEMENT

conclusion is reached in the Johannine literature. Yet unsatisfactory as this method is, it is less so than the kind of simplification which takes some particular idea, such as the Kingdom of God, makes it theologically and religiously central, and brings all else into an unreal subordination to it except for the elimination as irrelevant of intractable material.

Approach the question along a different path. What is the most striking fact about New Testament religion? I should be inclined to say its immense vitality. The river of God is full of water, and the Church moved on the current of a deep and mighty stream. It possessed a Gospel, or rather was possessed by one. And that Gospel was essentially creative. It made Christians, that third race of men, neither, because both, Jews and Gentiles, and inspired their religion, their theology, and their morals. And its creative character can equally well be described as its redemptive energy. The man who in Christ was a new creation was a redeemed man. To this corresponds the typical emphasis on salvation, which is God's answer through the Gospel, which is at once the message and the conveyance of salvation to the world's evil. Almost at the beginning of what is probably the earliest of all the New Testament books stand words which are nothing less than the revelation of the strength of primitive Christianity displayed in its victories in the mission field—" Knowing . . . how that our gospel came not unto you in word only, but also in power, and in the Holy Ghost, and in much assurance." [1] The replies which we find Origen [2] giving to Celsus's

[1] 1 Thess. i. 5.   [2] Cf c. Celsum 1. 46, iii 44.

attacks on the character of those who accepted the Gospel, whether as proclaimed by Christ Himself or as afterwards delivered by Christian teachers,—that even if they had been persons of evil life they did not remain so, is the implicit apologetic of the New Testament itself.

Now this creative element in the Gospel derives from the Cross as seen in the light of the Resurrection. The connexion is both a historical one and an ideal one, for the evidence which we possess does not allow us to suppose that the Cross was ever regarded or preached as no more than a great Jewish crime, religiously irrelevant. The way in which the Christian consciousness quite early fastened on Isaiah liii. as giving the prophetic interpretation of the Cross is proof of that, while the ideal or mystical connexion is suggested by the fact that as the Cross is the original divine paradox, so, in the working of the Gospel upon those who submit themselves to it, there is revealed a wisdom and a power which are not within the compass of the mighty and the learned of this world. The Cross is the divine paradox because it enshrines not the defeat but the victory of God. It is not outside the mystery of God's dealings with the world, but is their heart, since God's saving activity is there no longer a promise but an actual gift and power. So the Cross is the beginning of a new history of which the firstfruits are the moral transmutation and spiritual enrichment which come to pass in the Christian life.

But the recognition of all this does not mean that a full apprehension of the Cross is within our power. Many attempts have been made to unveil the Cross

THE ATONEMENT

in such a way as to show how it fulfils God's plan of world-salvation. And it cannot be said that any one doctrine or any harmonization of different doctrines lets us into the secret. The mystery of the Cross is not a completely revealed mystery. The light which streams out from it to lighten the path of those who walk in the way everlasting, which is the high road of the Gospel, so that *Via Crucis est Via Lucis*, leaves the Cross itself in a shadow which dims its outlines. There is not, either in the New Testament or in the theology of the Church, a perfect rationalization of its value.

I think we may see how this is, if we make use of a conception round which Professor Otto has written his remarkable book, *The Idea of the Holy*. He insists that that idea is not exhausted in its meaning when interpreted as the morally good. There is something "extra," something which involves an emotional feeling of awe and of fascination on the part of the self, conscious of the fact that it is in the presence of an inexpressible mystery. To the object which arouses such feelings Dr. Otto gives the title "numinous," formed from numen, the Latin word for Deity, while the experience which it evokes he describes as numinous emotion or consciousness. It is not that the ethical element in the holy is non-essential, but, in Dr. Otto's words, the term "holy" "includes in addition . . . a clear overplus of meaning."[1] And both in the Old Testament and in the New he finds important illustrations of this numinous feeling.

Now it is exceedingly likely that this book will be much abused by those who will see in it another pile of

[1] p. 5.

handy stones which they can throw at that rational element in life and thought which excites, as Dr. Inge many years ago pointed out,[1] such curious and intense hostility in certain quarters. And though Professor Otto himself is so far from being an enemy of the development of rational ideas that he can write: " the process of rationalization and moralization of the numinous, as it grows ever more clear and more potent, is in fact the most essential part of what we call 'Sacred History' and prize as the ever-growing self-revelation of the divine,"[2] I am not sure that he has always sufficiently guarded against the danger. But however that may be, I would suggest that the Cross, to which he does not refer—he is nearest to it when he speaks of Christ's Agony in Gethsemane—comes very close to his conception of a numinous object, and that the feeling-response to it is not simply trust and love, but a sense of awe and fascination. It is Christ lifted up on the Cross Who draws men unto Himself; doctrines of the Atonement may even be prejudicial to this by an excessive or false rationalization, an admission which is decidedly not a plea for the abandonment of the rational and doctrinal element. But when St. Paul[3] speaks of the Father's good pleasure " to reconcile all things unto Himself through the blood of His cross; through Him, I say, whether things upon the earth or things in heaven "; when St. Peter[4] describes the angels as desiring to look into the prophetic announcements of " the sufferings of

[1] In *Personal Idealism and Mysticism.*
[2] p 115
[3] 1 Col 1 20.
[4] 1 St Peter 1. 10–12.

THE ATONEMENT

Christ and the glories that should follow them"; when the seer of the Apocalypse [1] sees in the midst of the heavenly worshippers "a Lamb standing as though it had been slain"; or when, to take one notable example from the history of Christian devotion, great mystics and ascetics like St. Francis and Thomas à Kempis and Lady Julian of Norwich have poured themselves out in adoration and service of Him Who was to them, in an overwhelming reality, the crucified Lord Jesus, and Thomas Traherne extolled the Cross as "the abyss of wonders, the centre of desires, the school of virtues, the house of wisdom, the throne of love, the theatre of joys, and the place of sorrows," [2] we are conscious of the inspiration of a deep and mysterious reality to which the reason by itself never could do justice, a reality whose holiness is something more than moral perfection. And if, as all Christians would agree, the Cross does in a unique way reveal the love of God, we see perhaps how this must be, for the love of God is that perfection of His being which cannot be identified either with intensity of feeling or with activity of benevolence. Though I could not claim his authority for my use of the expression which meant so much to him, I would emphasise with Dr. Forsyth the truth that God's love is holy love.

But perhaps we can take a step further. When we try, as we must, to illuminate and interpret the Cross by the introduction of moral ideas, those ideas represent the category of the holy on its rational side. Yet

[1] Apoc v. 6
[2] Quoted by Mrs Herman in *The Meaning and Value of Mysticism*, p. 211.

those ideas themselves are not purely rational. Take any of the great words which have been used to illuminate the shadow in which the Cross stands, such words as expiation, satisfaction, substitution, representation, and remember that behind all these words is implied the existence of a moral world-order. Can one handle these as though they were, in the context in which they are employed, perfectly rational conceptions? Whichever we choose, does there not remain an element of unsolved mystery? In such a restatement of Abelard's view that the Cross saves by its power to call forth love and penitence, as we possess in the Bampton Lectures of the late Dean Rashdall, we have, through the omission of all idea of a relation of the Cross to a moral world-order, a rationalized doctrine of the Atonement which does indeed avoid all the difficulties which rise up when we try to show how the death of Christ has an expiatory value in respect of sin and a propitiatory value towards God, or when, if we prefer another, not necessarily opposed, category, we say that Christ died as the representative of humanity. But the simplicity of Dr. Rashdall's view, while it has its attraction owing to its intellectual lucidity, is really its weakness. It is not easy to analyse all the elements which make up an act of all-grateful adoration, but I do not think that the response of the Christian heart to Christ crucified would ever normally be content to translate the meaning of its feelings into the acknowledgment—I quote Dr. Rashdall—that " the voluntary death of the innocent Son of God on man's behalf moves the sinner to gratitude and answering love—and so to consciousness of sin, repentance,

THE ATONEMENT

amendment." The first twelve words of the sentence are unexceptionable, and almost every believer in the Atonement, in any sense, would make them his own, but unfortunately the words that follow throw all the stress on what man is to do in respect of his own salvation, while the death on man's behalf is not, in the interpretation, allowed to transcend, except in degree, even though a superlative one, the service which a righteous man can render by his death. Whatever criticisms may be valid against theories, or aspects of theories, of objective atonement, a doctrine which would interpret the true meaning of the worship of Jesus as the Saviour within the limits of the above sentence is not likely to satisfy the Christian appreciation of the wonder and the grace of the Cross.

Moreover, we must not ignore the relevance of the Catholic doctrine of the Incarnation. There may be a certain formality in the way in which Anselm argues from the infinite value of Christ's Person to the infinite value of His death. But behind that lies the very strong religious instinct which finds expression in St. Paul's address to the Ephesian elders on the Westcott and Hort reading of Acts xx. 28—"The Church of God which He purchased with His own blood," which appears in Ignatius's intense desire to be allowed to become an imitator of the suffering of his God (Rom. 6), to which the Patripassian and Theopaschite controversies bear witness, and which in our own days has shown itself in the discussions concerning "a suffering God"—a strong instinct for emphasizing the experience of the Passion as the experience of God. With whatever doctrinal defects, sometimes serious ones, a real religious value must be recognized as manifesting itself at this point. In the Person of the Son God Himself penetrates the life of the world, its suffering, its evil. He holds back nothing. True, He maintains through it all His absolute holiness of being and energy, but He maintains it not aloof from but at close quarters with the world's evil. He draws the sting of evil by letting it appear to defeat Him, and thereby gaining an irreversible victory. The Cross is the source of the new moral creation, because in it every moral need is met and satisfied. It is a finished work. And it is the satisfaction of those needs which the great words of the Atonement theology are intended to express.

Accordingly, we shall say that if the Christian Gospel reveals in an unparalleled way the holiness of God, and reveals it with such fullness as is possible in the world's life, it is to the Cross that we must turn our eyes in order to see it most perfectly given. The holiness of the Crucified was the one adequate response from within the world to the holiness of God. It was, as McLeod Campbell said, " A perfect Amen in humanity to the judgment of God on the sin of man." [1] It was because He did no sin that He could bear our sins in His own body on the tree. And while no theory can do justice to such words as these, or to others which enable us to catch the accents of the apostolic preaching of the messages of salvation, that is not because those theories in which the worship of Christ crucified took intellectual shape, and the New Testament Gospel was set forth in a system of rational notions, possessed no real depth

[1] *The Nature of the Atonement*, p. 116.

THE ATONEMENT

and permanence, and were merely relative to the ages in which they severally appeared, and to those ages' thought-forms, but because in the Cross and in the moral order which the Cross re-creates there is an overplus incapable of rationalization. We cannot hope for a final doctrine of the Atonement. There will always be a shadow round the Cross. But that shadow, as it does not check the adoration of the heart, so it does not forbid the activity of the mind. Knowledge is possible, if but in part, and vision if only as through a glass darkly. And what we see and know is the new created at the cost which the old entailed, the cost of the precious Blood of Christ shed for the world's redemption, and to the mystery of the malignancy of evil opposing the greater mystery of dying and triumphant holiness. And that, after all, is a gospel rather than a doctrine or a theology—but a gospel creative of Christian theology because it is a gospel creative of Christian men.

II

THE MEANING OF CALVARY

I

THE simplest things in life are the most tremendous, and the things we most take for granted the most mysterious. Yet it is wise sometimes to think about these simple things, these foundation facts. For these are the final mysteries, and when you meet a final mystery you are on a road which leads straight through (though it may be a long road and slow) to God.

And as with life itself, so with what you can say about life. There is a grand simplicity about the judgments which we think it really worth while to pass. We are not so much concerned (perhaps we should be more) with the art-critics and the philosophers. But it is not easy to keep pace with them, and they often speak as experts to experts. Our final judgments are ours in virtue of our common humanity and its experiences, and when we express them we express them in terms of good and evil. Beyond those terms we cannot pass. Doubtless we need educating in our moral judgments. But there is no meaning in talk about a sphere beyond good and evil. We have and can have no knowledge, or power of conceiving of, such a sphere. Remember those words which Mr. Chesterton makes Father Brown address to the sham priest, who is really the great criminal Flambeau, intent upon the theft of the Blue

THE MEANING OF CALVARY

Cross: "Think of forests of adamant with leaves of brilliants. Think the moon is a blue moon, a single elephantine sapphire. But don't fancy that all that frantic astronomy would make the smallest difference to the reason and justice of conduct. On plains of opal, under cliffs cut out of pearl, you would still find a notice-board, 'Thou shalt not steal.'"

And so of life : its final values are its moral values : and of our judgments, none are so simple, so inevitable, but so penetrative to within the very core of life's meaning as those which are based on our recognition of the distinction between good and evil.

But it is not just a distinction : it is a clash and tension of a unique kind. That is revealed in the world's history, and the issue of it becomes the world's judgment. Nay, more, if the clash and tension have reached a point beyond which it is impossible for them to go, if the world's moral history can be found somewhere condensed into a moment, the whole issue between good and evil made plain, and not only made plain, but passing to a final judgment, which is God's, and not only passing to final judgment, but crowned with a victory which can never be undone, then you have the solution of the problem which is the decision of the battle. One real decision in the warfare between good and evil is enough : for one real decision there holds the reversion of all eternity and settles for ever the question of world-mastery. Only, do not let us imagine that such a decision can be easy, or lack much foreboding and pain for whoever comes to its test and passes within its unsparing gloom. "Remove this cup from Me"; "Now is My soul troubled ; and what shall I say? Father, save Me from this hour." At such a crisis, only that perfect unity of the will with God, that "Howbeit, not what I will but what Thou wilt," that "But for this cause came I unto this hour," will carry through to the end one upon whom the moral ends of all the ages have come. Only by taking the whole cost and redeeming it can he make the settlement and win the peace. It is the almighty deed, not any word however mighty, which secures the judgment of this world and the casting out of its prince. "I, if I be lifted up from the earth, will draw all men unto Myself."

II

This vision of the world is, for the Christian, inseparable from his vision of God. For unity here he draws deeply upon the New Testament at its deepest. The theology of the New Testament is throughout a moral theology. It is comparatively little concerned with many speculative problems which vexed men's minds while its books were being written, and vex them still. But when you come to persons and personal relationships, especially the relationship between persons and a world of persons and the God Who, whatever else He is, is anyhow as personal as we are, you read something quite final spread out before you. What is it that is distinctive of the New Testament's handling of evil? This—that the evil which makes the difference is not to be looked for outside but within the action of personal wills, and that its real meaning is to be found only as you look at it in contrast with God. God, the God of all holiness and love, has His holy and loving

THE MEANING OF CALVARY 59

purposes for the world. Those purposes are the best purposes possible, final correspondence with the will of God and peace in its attainment. And evil, as the opposition to those purposes, as the reaction of will against Will, is treason to the one possible highest good. It is sin against God, the destructive force whose triumph would mean the extinction of all true moral values from the universe, the twilight and passing of God. That is the situation which the New Testament and historic Christianity face, a situation threatening disaster, and needing the strongest possible antidote to its own disease. And the most effective cure is a new creation which does not simply pass over the old as though it did not exist (a method of no moral value), but deals with it according to its merits and needs, which is the method of judgment, and yet uses judgment for salvation and restores while it re-creates.

What we need to grasp, what the New Testament would have us grasp, as the key to the whole matter, is that God deals with the issue raised by moral evil and with its consequences for His world by His own intimate and costly personal action. We begin to understand only as we confess that the whole initiative is His. In the coming of Christ God makes His nearest approach to the world and to its sin. In creation He acts upon the world from without; in redemption He acts upon it from within. He gives Himself fully in the one as He had not done in the other. And so He reveals more of Himself. We know more of the Blessed Trinity through the work of the Son in His mission and death, than we could ever know through the work of that same Son in the framing of the worlds. We see better and more truly because we see more that is finished. There was a finished work of God, greater and more complete, when Christ died upon the Cross than when God rested on the seventh day from all the works which He had created and made. It is this finished work which we describe as atonement. I would press that point. What is the meaning of the Cross? Why did the coming of Christ find its climax in the death of Christ? Why is there more of God's grace in Christ's Cross than of man's sin (which is huge enough), and more of God's grace in that Cross than in any of Christ's gracious words and mighty deeds? For I do not think that there can be any doubt that the New Testament and Christian experience both bring us to the same conclusion and certainty.

Aware as I am, as anyone must be, of the dangers of brevity and condensation at this point, I will try first to condense the answer and then to give some exposition of it. And the answer itself I would give in these words—Christ on the Cross accepts God's judgment upon man, and expresses God's judgment upon sin. He accepts. For such acceptance was the one thing that a guilty world should offer to God, were it able to offer that. The only way in which the inhabitants of the world can begin to learn righteousness when God's judgments are abroad, is by accepting those judgments against themselves, and by bearing witness, "Righteous art Thou, O Lord, who judgest." If a guilty world could expiate its own offences and make itself fit to receive the divine forgiveness, it would be by bowing its head under the

THE MEANING OF CALVARY

divine judgments, and letting God have His way with it. And He who was made one with His brethren in their nature was made one with His brethren in their sin. He was made sin—He the Holy One in Whom the Father was for ever well-pleased—made one with sinners in that most awful of all identifications. He spared not Himself, so that He might help us to the uttermost. Everything fell on Him, disappointment, apparent failure, cowardice, treachery, torture, death. Everything seemed to fall away from Him, even the light of His Father's countenance. Had He been a sinner, what more was there for Him to expect and receive from men and God? What bitterer cup to drink? "Lo, I come to do Thy will, O God." That was His way in the world, His way to the end. He did that will, while he endured all that it brought upon Him, brought upon Him not arbitrarily, nor vindictively, nor as though that will ever did or could stand in any sort of hostile relationship to Him. Such an idea, could anyone hold it, would be moral insanity. Yet God's controversy with a sinful world could not cease because His Only Son had stepped within the borders of the world, nor could the Son be isolated from the incessant reaction of the Divine holiness, expressing itself in judgment upon the world. But what the Son did was a new thing, and what the Father beheld was a new thing, the whole-hearted acceptance of judgment in willing sacrifice, and in the blood outpoured for the forgiveness of those sins whose burden He took. And so the chastisement of our peace was upon Him. He did for us what we never could have done; but it was a work of no private interest or restricted range. For He is greater than the world, as its Redeemer, and not only as its Creator, and as He accepts God's judgments upon the world, so He creates the world afresh to God, and as the Head of the new humanity binds all men by a closer tie to Himself.

But there is more even than this. In the Cross of Christ judgment is not only accepted, but delivered. Christ works against sin even while he puts Himself within the power of the judgment which it inevitably brings. His death is the condemnation of sin. The judgment which He accepts from God because of sin is at the same time God's final judgment upon sin. The Cross is that bruising of the head of the serpent from which there is no recovery. The adequate confession of God's holiness is the shaming of sin and the breaking of its power. That old idea of the devil outreaching himself in the death of Christ, and so compassing his own destruction, is in substance, whatever it be in form, much more than a piece of curious mythology. It bears witness to the triumphant side of the Cross, to that counter-destructiveness which outmatches the destructiveness of sin. If sin is ever really judged, it is thereby, in its root and in its final issues, rendered impotent. All such judgment is the judgment of God. In a world of moral realities and values, there is and can be no such thing as self-acting judgment which is not at the same time the judgment of God.

And so the cloud of sin is lifted off the world. The old passes away; it is atoned and reconciled, and the new order takes its place. Reconciliation without

THE MEANING OF CALVARY

atonement would not do justice to God, and so not to man. Atonement stands for that linking of sin with judgment which is the penal consequence of sin. There is no disparagement of God's free forgiveness here. Who would dare to say that God has ever failed to forgive freely one who truly repented? But the forgiveness of sins is part of the moral world-order and not the whole of it. It works individually, and God's moral relationship to the world is more than, and indeed different from, a set of particular individual relationships. Those continue in process of completion, and sin and forgiveness go to their unmaking and remaking. It is against the background of a reconciled world that the appeal to the individual goes forth. God has in Christ reconciled the world to Himself, and so "Be ye reconciled with God." That is the true Christian order, and the only one which does full justice to the Cross in the whole economy of Christian thought and life.

III

But if all this is ascribed to the Cross, where is the special triumph of the Resurrection? Is it not left rather as an epilogue than as a relevant part of Christ's great work? Let me quote you an old thought of Mr. H. G. Wells,[1] and not at all one of his happiest ones, that we may see at least what we have to avoid:

"When I think of the Resurrection I am always reminded of the 'happy endings' that editors and actor managers are accustomed to impose upon essentially tragic novels and plays. . . ."

[1] *First and Last Things*, p. 88.

Wherever he got that thought he did not get it from the New Testament. The New Testament knows nothing whatever about an essentially tragic story which is converted into something else for the benefit of a number of third parties. And where the writer is from the point of view of the New Testament utterly at fault, is that while the Resurrection reminds him of an ending, it is in that original literature quite regularly acclaimed as a beginning. It is not the end of anything at all. It is the first manifestation of the new order which has been brought into existence by Jesus Christ. He is its creator, and it is first manifested through the manifestation of Him. Nor is the Resurrection a reversal of a tragedy ; it, with the Ascension that follows, is the crowning of a victory. The fact is that there is a straight line through in the Gospels to the Cross and the Resurrection and beyond. You can see that in the way our Lord spoke of the things that were to befall Him ; there is no sharp distinction made between the Passion and the rising again. We suffer more than a little from unreal dislocations in our theology, and even in our practical religion. The Incarnation, the Cross, and the Resurrection go together ; they make up one living, concrete whole, and as a whole offer themselves to Christian belief and experience. Nevertheless, I would say this. I believe that our theology of recent years has suffered some real harm through a lack of emphasis on the fact of the Resurrection. For that is a fact which we ought not to ignore in our interpretation of the Gospel records as a whole, while the whole of our Christian profession is illuminated when it is

THE MEANING OF CALVARY

consciously linked with Him Whose priesthood stands, as the writer to the Hebrews puts it, in the power of an indissoluble life.

We live in no easy world. It has its gifts and joys, but also much that seems to frustrate the one and to overshadow the other. The adjustment to it of those who are counted most fortunate has neither mark of perfection nor promise of permanency. Nor in itself does it move forward to moral victory. But to the Christian believer that is but the outside of the matter. He knows that the real order is the redeemed order of the new creation, which the Holy Father established in His Son and has destined for eternity. All that truly belongs to it abides for ever. Sorrows and disappointments and losses may fall on those who share in it; nor are they, because they have a part in its holiness, thereby escaped from all sin. We may think of it as the Church; we may think of it as the Kingdom. But always it is the restored Garden and Paradise regained, and the Tree of Life which stands at its centre and round which it grows is the Tree of judgment and salvation, the Cross of our Lord and Saviour Jesus Christ.

III
THE THEOLOGY OF DR. FORSYTH

THE death of the Principal of Hackney College has bereft English Christianity of its most powerful, its most challenging, and, perhaps, its actually greatest theologian in the sphere of dogmatics. During the last fifteen years he had come more and more to be recognized as occupying a position of almost solitary eminence. That is not to say that he has at any time been appreciated at his true worth. His mind and the *Zeitgeist* have never marched in sympathy. What he said of the theological passages in his *Religion in Recent Art*[1] may be applied much more widely. He lived not only in an age when serious theology was always handicapped owing to the general trend of the popular taste, but in an age which, in so far as it was interested in theology at all, liked something very different from what Forsyth could or would give it. The public has tastes and likings in theology. Forsyth had neither (though one must admit that he had their negatives), and to speak of " liking " a book of his has almost an absurd sound. An American once put it in that downright way which seems to come natural to the Far Western mind—" You either swear with Peter Taylor Forsyth or you swear at him." But even to swear at him it was necessary to understand him more adequately than was common. I

[1] Hodder & Stoughton, 1905, p. xi f.

THE THEOLOGY OF DR. FORSYTH

noticed that in one or two notices of him, after his death, *The Christian Ethic of War*[1] was picked out for particular comment. In that book his mind did move in agreement with the general opinion of the time. But one may question whether readers or reviewers who delighted in his belabouring of the pacificists had much appreciation of the theological ethic which armed him in what, without doubt, he regarded as part of the Lord's controversy. Some at least probably fell within the criticism of the note on page 140 of the book :—" It is odd that some of the most ' tender ' exponents of a sentimental religion are among the most belligerent critics of the pacifists they have been making for many years."

Nor was it only the theology, such as it was, of the popular level which had little in common with Forsyth's faith, and with his dogmatic construction grounded in faith's certainty and apprehension of the distinctive thing in God, and therefore in all religion and all life. Scientific theology, as a whole, was immersed in other interests and pursued other ends than his. This may be witnessed in three respects. First, there was and is the immense concentration of first-rate ability upon the critical issues raised in connexion with the New Testament. Of the value of the Higher Criticism Forsyth always wrote with great respect: " The service rendered to Christianity by the great critical movement is almost beyond words "[2]; but the special interest he had in it was due to his feeling that it had cleared the ground for the erection of a

[1] Longmans, 1916.
[2] *The Person of Jesus Christ*, p. viii (Congregational Union and Hodder & Stoughton, 1909.)

dogmatic edifice in which the component materials could be selected according to their real strength. Now this valuation of criticism in respect of the theological possibilities which it opens up, though not absent from the mind of the critics, is not habitually used as it was by Forsyth. The great critic is often far from being a great theologian : unfortunately, the distinction is not always well understood. It is much easier to be and to be recognized as a good critic than to gain well-merited fame as a good theologian. Had Forsyth done anything nearly as remarkable in critical work as he did in theology he would have made a name for himself far more easily and widely. Secondly, the one dogma (hardly indeed regarded as such) which had, partly as a result of one great phase of criticism, partly owing to other causes, come to the front and laid some real hold on the public mind, was that of the Fatherhood of God. Now against this dogma *in the way in which it was held* Forsyth was in continual opposition. He must have seemed to be, and to some extent he was, unsympathetic and even harsh. Yet all the time a most profound sense of the reality of God's Fatherhood underlay his reaction from the popular conception. But for him it was no solitary and easily accessible dogma, but a triumph of faith, working on its grasp of moral realities and steadying itself by its still stronger grasp of Christ. The impression left is very different from that made in Harnack's famous lectures on *Das Wesen des Christentums*, and prolonged in those who gave Harnack a ready welcome. Theological liberalism and popular sympathies found themselves in close alliance ; the

THE THEOLOGY OF DR. FORSYTH 69

same fire cheered them with its pleasant warmth; and Forsyth was out in the cold. And then, finally, the theology which had passed further along and put Christ in the centre, with a firm belief that in Christ Himself was to be found the key to true theology, so that Christology could not be treated as a matter of subordinate moment, was greatly inclined to throw the emphasis on the Incarnation itself in such a way as to lessen the importance of the Atonement and to leave soteriology outside the centre of religious interests. This was certainly the case in the Church of England; both High Church and Broad Church tended in this direction. I do not suppose that the case was exactly similar in the Free Churches, where the particular Catholic interest in the Incarnation was not to be looked for, but Forsyth's constant references to the perplexity which resulted from his characteristic soteriological emphases point to an analogous situation.

The fact is that Forsyth was eminently what the mind of his time, not least the Christian mind, needed, but not what it wanted. Dr. Hamilton in a review of *Lectures on the Church and the Sacraments*[1] in the *Journal of Theological Studies*, and I think it was Dr. Andrews, in one of the tributes to Forsyth published in the *British Weekly*, both spoke of him as a prophet. And so he was: but he was always a theological prophet, or, better still, a prophetic theologian, a fact which Dr. Hamilton failed to realize. It was as a theologian, with all the theologian's apparatus and the standards of judgment which the theologian is bound

[1] Longmans, 1917.

to employ, that he challenged contemporary tendencies. At a time when there was much talk of revised theologies, new theologies, and so forth, he was concerned to point out that a real knowledge of theology was indispensable for a revision of theology. Here is a passage from *Positive Preaching and Modern Mind*,[1] which gives his mind on this point and will show why he was never likely to have a great popular following: —" A man speaking his genuine experience in the experimental region of religion is always worth listening to. But if a man takes leave to assault the great doctrines, or to raise the great questions as if they had occurred to him first, if he knows nothing of what has been done in them by experts, or where thinkers have left the question, he is out of place. No man is entitled to discuss theology in public who has not studied theology. It is like any other weighty subject. Still more is this requisite if he set out to challenge and reform theology. He ought to be a trained theologian." It will always be necessary for someone to speak like this, bluntly and decisively; in so doing he renders a service both to the cause of truth and to his own generation. But he will have to pay for it in the absence of the applause and the fame which can be the lot of those whose theology is sometimes suggestive of more lack than surplus.[2] Dr. Forsyth was careless of popular enthusiasm, and did not court it. Before his life's work closed his reputation among those best qualified to judge was firmly established; and yet I am convinced that

---

[1] Hodder & Stoughton, 1907, p 102.
[2] ὑστέρημα—περίσσευμα, see 2 Cor. viii 14.

THE THEOLOGY OF DR. FORSYTH

even in favourable quarters his greatness as a theologian is not duly recognized.

Here is the place to say a word concerning his style. It has been severely criticized, and without doubt it was an additional barrier to the ordinary mind which wished to come in touch with him. The Free Church scholar who contributes to the *Manchester Guardian* over the letters "G. J." was particularly severe. Yet there is another side to the question. There was a challenging note about the style as there was about the thought, and there was a certain fitness in the sheer difficulties, sometimes amounting almost to antinomies, of what Forsyth had to say, being reflected in the literary instrument. What Forsyth said of St. Paul may not unfairly be reapplied to Forsyth himself:— "To express a reality so unspeakable he strained language and tortured ideas, which he enlisted from any quarter where he could lay hands on them."[1] I can believe that he felt of almost every one of his books that it was a battle in which he had to use every means available for arresting his reader's mind and compelling him to attend. Even as tactics that may often have been a mistake, for beyond a certain point epigram and antithesis weary and do not stimulate. But the real and final truth is that his style became part of himself and was not detachable at will. Forsyth was not a man with a bad (or brilliant, or remarkable) style; but the style was Forsyth on paper.

In passing to some description of Dr. Forsyth's theology, a certain difficulty confronts the writer

[1] *Positive Preaching*, p. 18.

from the fact that any sort of organized treatment purporting to represent Dr. Forsyth's positions as so many points in a dogmatic system is almost sure to introduce an impression of logical coherence and orderly advance more formal than the writings themselves warrant. It is true that every one of the great problems of theology proper, and many which arise in connexion with its presuppositions and premises, are faced and handled in those writings; but there is something almost incidental in the way in which such a doctrine as that of the Trinity now and then appears, while the Atonement itself which, as viewed by him in its relation to the moral world, forms the background of the thought, and never a mere scenic background of (is it an exaggeration to say?) every page he wrote, was never the subject of a formal theological treatise. That character belongs to not more than three of his books, and to them not completely, to *The Principle of Authority*,[1] in which Forsyth's theory of knowledge and philosophy of religion are set forth; to *The Justification of God*,[2] which contains his treatment of the great and pressing theme of Theodicy; and to *The Person and Place of Jesus Christ*, the most orderly and the greatest of all his works. What I propose to do is to subdivide the general subject of Forsyth's theology into five sections, to try to do some justice to the main lines of his thought in each one, and to show how the controlling ideas of one section lead on naturally to the dogmatic conclusions of the next.

[1] Hodder & Stoughton, 1912.
[2] Duckworth, 1916.

THE THEOLOGY OF DR. FORSYTH

I

Let us start with his theory of knowledge, which involves his philosophy of religion and the idea of God. Here Forsyth stands on the side of the voluntarists as against the intellectualists. But his voluntarism was of the Kantian and not of the later pragmatic kind. He was immensely concerned with the real as something given, and he found it given in the ethical. Where there is action there is ethic, and man cannot help acting. "The last reality, and that with which every man willy-nilly has to do, is not a reality of thought, but of life, and of conscience, and of judgment. We are in the world to act and take the consequences. Action means and matters everything in the world."[1] Accordingly Kant was on the right lines when he started the movement as a result of which "the ethical took the place that had been held by the intellectual. The notion of reality replaced that of truth. Religion placed us not in line with the rationality of the world but in rapport with the reality of it. And the ethical was the real."[2] Where Modernism has gone far wrong is in the weakness of its ethical knowledge.[3] Of the existence of forms of thought and rational ideas latent in the mind in abstraction from concrete, historical experiences he is entirely sceptical: "the fact is, as I say, we have no forms of knowledge which are not produced by particular contacts and experiences in ourselves or the race."[4]

[1] *The Cruciality of the Cross*, p. 121, Hodder & Stoughton, 1909.
[2] *Principle of Authority*, p. 5.
[3] Ibid., p. 78 f.
[4] Ibid., p. 107.

But how do we know what experiences we may rely upon as giving us the key to the final meaning and character of the universe? How are we to escape subjectivism, and come by a reality universally valid, in which the intellect as well as the will may find itself at home? How are we to be sure about the content of experience? Forsyth's answer is that such certainty is unattainable out of our natural selves. Certainty can come only through an invasive authority which lifts us on to a higher level. Certainty can exist only if there is such a thing as revelation, and that which answers to revelation is faith. Faith is "an organ of real knowledge," [1] but faith is itself "the gift and creation of God." [2] His thought at this point might be taken as exegetical of Irenæus's saying, *impossibile est sine Deo discere Deum*. A saying of St. Paul's to which he more than once recurs as putting us on the right lines for the understanding of the principle of religious knowledge is Gal. iv. 9, "but now that ye have come to know God or rather to be known of God." So in religion "our knowledge relates not to an object but to a subject who takes the initiative, not to what we reach but to what reaches us, not to something we know but to someone who knows us. It is knowledge not of a known thing but of a knowing God." [3] And the seat of the relationship set up in this knowledge of man by God and man's answering knowledge of God is to be looked for in the region of the will and conscience. And in that region, being known by God means being

---

[1] *Positive Preaching*, p 250.
[2] *Principle of Authority*, p. 30.
[3] Ibid , p. 102.

THE THEOLOGY OF DR. FORSYTH

saved and re-created by God, since the man who finds himself faced by the demands of a moral universe with which his sin brings him into collision can find no sure footing for his soul except as he finds it in a redemption "commensurate with the Sanctity, the Majesty, the rock Reality of things."[1]

Knowledge, then, is the apprehension of the real. And the real is primarily the ethical and finally the redemptive. It is in redemption that we become certain of revelation and of authority. "Revelation would be impossible, it would be mere exhibition, it would not get home, were it not also, in the same act, Redemption and Regeneration."[2] And that which is absolutely authoritative is that which is absolutely holy. Such authority is "the new-creative action of the perfectly holy conscience of God on the helplessly guilty conscience of man."[3]

Two obvious objections can be made to this line of thought. The first is that whatever the individual experiences for himself there is no valid reason why he should ascribe to that experience a more than subjective value, no means whereby he can universalize it as something expressive of a relationship with God, which is the most real relationship in which the whole world can stand to God. With this objection Forsyth twice deals, drawing a distinction, which takes us some way, between experience and the content of experience.[4] The second objection is that if knowledge is bound up with redemption, and redemption is the act of God,

[1] *Principle of Authority*, p. 206.
[2] Ibid., p. 30
[3] Ibid., p. 65.
[4] Ibid., pp. 29–31, 91–93.

"natural" knowledge of God is impossible and argument is useless. Forsyth frankly allows, indeed insists, that " a real objective, the certainty of a transcendent reality, we reach only by something in the nature of miracle, something donated and invasive from the living God. Only so do we reach the conviction, so essential for religion, of a reality totally independent of ourselves,"[1] and he appeals to Troeltsch and Eucken in support. And I do not see how we either can or can want to evade this conclusion. If the knowledge of God is a religious act we cannot keep God out of the act of our knowing Him. That kind of Pelagianism, like every other, is inadmissible. But we are not therefore compelled to think of God's revelation of Himself in redeeming action as partial and magical, nor of men as mere passive instruments. Dr. Forsyth, like Dr. Oman, never looks for any other relationships between God and man except personal relationships. God does not and cannot treat persons as things. Accordingly if in revelation and redemption he sees, as he does see, miracle, it is not miracle coercive of the soul's natural freedom. "Faith is the soul believing. Its creation can only be some action appropriate to soul—i.e. to freedom. Redemption is recreating a free soul through its freedom. It is converting its freedom, and not its substance."[2]

What we secure in religious knowledge (and though the action of the will is emphasized, the place of the intellect, though secondary, is not denied—even if "many have so learned Kant"[3]) is the certainty of a

[1] *Principle of Authority*, p. 171 f.
[2] Ibid., p. 179.
[3] Ibid., p. 116.

God able to bring the human conscience and will into harmony with a universe of which the last reality is moral, a God able to deal with that profoundly ethical and tragic side of life which realists like Ibsen and Carlyle force us to face.[1] Such is the God given to us in the Gospel, and in the Gospel we have God's method of dealing with the situation created by the clash between good and evil, by that subversion of the moral order which results from sin and by mankind's need of a salvation which it cannot effect by its own resources. The Gospel answers to the situation by being concrete, historic, and ethical. It deals, of necessity, with humanity as a whole. " Humanity is not a mere mass of units. It is an organism with a history. And revelation therefore is God's treatment of us *in a history*, in a Humanity. . . . If God's treatment of us be redemptive, it is a historic redemption. Its content is the living, loving, saving God ; its compass is cosmic, its sphere is human history, actual history."[2] In the Gospel we see the interaction of those two truths which Forsyth used to assert, Butler's " Morality is the nature of things," and Augustine's *Bonitas est substantia Dei*. The Gospel, then, as Forsyth understood and expressed it, claims our attention in the second section.

II

But the problem of authority is still with us. For what is the Gospel, and what is the source of our certitude as to it ? Here we come into sight of posi-

[1] See the remarkable pages specially devoted to Ibsen's moral insight and blindness in *Positive Preaching*, pp 150–2.

[2] *Hibbert Journal*, **x.** 1 (October, 1911), art. " Revelation and Bible," p. 241.

tions from which, at least from the year 1905, Forsyth never varied, and which belong to the very essence of his theology. On the one hand he had to reckon with the Catholic insistence on the authority of the Church, on the other on the Protestant assertion of the infallibility of the Bible. He rejected both these solutions of the problem. The critical movement had destroyed the doctrine of verbal inerrancy; while greatly as he exalted the idea of the Church, the Church was not for him the extension of the Incarnation, it could not be identified with any one existing society, and the letter of the Creeds was no more final than the letter of Scripture. But he did not, in breaking with what had come to be regarded as Protestant orthodoxy at this point, and in refusing the Catholic alternative, go over to the Liberals with their reduction of the whole authoritarian idea, and constant vagueness as to what the really fundamental thing in Christianity is. Forsyth went behind both Bible and Church to that which was the soul and the creator of them both, to the Gospel of God's redeeming grace in Christ. "Remember," he says, " that Christ did not come to bring a Bible but to bring a Gospel. The Bible arose afterwards from the Gospel to serve the Gospel. . . . The Bible, the preacher, and the Church are all made by the same thing—the Gospel."[1] This Gospel was preeminently God's action, His treatment in Christ of the world's moral tragedy, God's revelation of Himself breaking in upon the world as redemption. It is this which runs through the New Testament κήρυγμα and forms its great content, and it is this which the Church

[1] *Positive Preaching*, p 15.

THE THEOLOGY OF DR. FORSYTH

is concerned with in its dogma: "Dogma is final revelation in germinal statement. It is God's act put as truth. It is the expression of the original and supernatural *datum* of the purely given which creates religion. It is truth about that in God which the Church stands upon. It is primary theology, or the Church's *footing*—as in John iii. 16."[1]

But how can we know that this account of the Gospel, this interpretation of it in terms of God's gracious and saving action in Christ, is the true one? For other accounts have been given. There is Hegel's conception of Christianity as the most perfect unfolding of the true and absolute Idea, of Christian dogmatic as the religious expression of abstract truth, especially in connexion with the doctrine of the Trinity. There is the attempt, often associated with the name of Harnack, to find a residual Gospel in the teaching of Jesus about the Fatherhood of God and the brotherhood of man. Can we not be content with something like the latter, and sit loose to anything more "dogmatic"? To answer such questions, Forsyth pointed to the New Testament as a whole. He insisted that a common Gospel of God's saving work in Christ dominates the New Testament writers, and that no other Gospel can be found there, and he appealed to the conclusions of recent competent New Testament scholarship—"Schlatter on the right, Feine in the centre, or Weinel on the left. The whole work, also, of the brilliant religious-historical school in the last dozen years has gone to show a substantial dogmatic unity in the Gospel of the first Church. . . . There was, of course,

[1] *Theology in Church and State*, Hodder & Stoughton, 1915, p. 12 f.

no universal theological formula, there was not an orthodoxy; but certainly there was a common Apostolic Gospel, a κήρυγμα." [1] But, supposing this is allowed, was this Gospel the true one; ought the Apostles to have preached it; may they not have misinterpreted and misrepresented Jesus? In answering this objection Forsyth does what I believe to be not only some of his most important work, but work badly needed and surprisingly neglected. The question of apostolic authority is a pressing one: it comes up in connexion with controversies of an institutional character, concerning the Church and the ministry, but it does not seem to emerge when the theological issue is raised, or, at least, it is not handled with due sense of its importance. Forsyth realized its immense importance, and not only with reference to St. Paul. He was no latter-day Marcion distinguishing between an inspired Paul and a mistaken Twelve; but he did face as regards the whole apostolic body the question which Marcion faced as regards St. Paul—have we here a true interpretation of Christ? There is a relevant section in *Theology in Church and State* [2] where the treatment is of that incisive, challenging character whereby Forsyth, whatever defects of style otherwise embarrassed his work, was able to make great issues plain :—" The Epistles are more inspired than the Gospels. We are in more direct contact with Christ. We are at one remove only. We hear the man who had Christ's own interpretation of His work. . . . The Gospels, with their unspeakable value, are yet but

[1] *Principle of Authority*, p 141.
[2] pp. 30–2.

THE THEOLOGY OF DR. FORSYTH

propædeutic to the Epistles; and most of the higher pains and troubles of the Church to-day arise from the displacement of its centre of gravity to the Gospels." But for his fullest mind on the matter one must go to the fifth and sixth lectures in *The Person and Place of Jesus Christ*. There the inspiration of the Apostles is viewed as the power which they possessed through charisma of the Spirit for the interpretation of the fact of Christ. " Apostolic inspiration, therefore, is a certain action stirred by the heavenly Christ in the soul, by which His first elect were enabled to see the moral, spiritual, and theological nature of the manifestation with a unique clearness, a clearness and explicitness perhaps not always present to Christ's own mind in doing the act." [1]

There is then a New Testament Gospel, and its centre is the Cross. So we approach the consideration of Forsyth's soteriology, wherein lies the greatest service he has done for the Church. But let us be clear about one thing at the start: Forsyth did not just reassert, with whatever power and insight, any one historic form of the doctrine of the Atonement. To understand him thus is to misunderstand him. He was no more wedded to the old categories in this respect than in any other. He asserts with great clearness and on more than one occasion the need for rejections and modifications. We must not speak about grace as procured by the Atonement, nor about the value of equivalent suffering, or even of suffering taken by itself, nor about

[1] *The Person and Place of Jesus Christ*, p. 176. Elsewhere Dr. Forsyth asks how, if the apostolic interpretation was wrong, it came about that Jesus had been unable to save them from so vast an error. does it not reflect on Him as a Teacher?

a change in God from wrath to grace, and we must be careful when we talk about substitution and penalty.[1] On the right and necessity of the progressive ethicizing of soteriological doctrine he is emphatic: "The whole great movement of thought on that question has been on an ascending moral scale. The more we modernize it the more we moralize it. And the modifications called for to-day are in the same direction."[2] But whereas some theologians, the more they ethicize, the less they seem to leave of anything that can be called Atonement at all, the very reverse is true of Forsyth, and that is no small part of the secret of his greatness in soteriology. The connexion stands out in words that follow almost immediately upon the previous quotation: "and it appears *en route* that we cannot ethicize Christianity without pursuing a doctrine of Atonement ever more positive. The more ethical we become the more exigent is holiness; and therefore the more necessary is Atonement as the action of love and grace at the instance of holiness and in its interests." Two words above all others lie at the heart of Forsyth's Atonement doctrine. They are "holiness" and "judgment." How often he recurs to the thought that the full truth is not that God is love, but that God is holy love. The whole moral crisis of things comes to a head in the opposition between God's holiness and the sin of the world. That we have to do with a God of holy love, that is the final truth of man's position. And where there is holiness, there must be judgment:

---

[1] See *The Cruciality of the Cross*, p. 78 f., pp. 191–3; *The Work of Christ*, Hodder & Stoughton, 1910, pp. 180–2.

[2] *Positive Preaching*, p. 294.

THE THEOLOGY OF DR. FORSYTH 83

"Do not think of God's judgment as an arbitrary infliction, but as the necessary reaction to sin in a holy God. There alone do you have the *divine* necessity of the Cross in a sinful world—the moral necessity of judgment."[1] It was this sense of the place of judgment and its sanctity which inspired the character of much of his treatment of the problem presented by the war, and ranged him so far on the other side from the pacificists.

But how was God's holiness honoured and His judgment delivered in the Cross? That is the question which many, I expect, are puzzled to find the answer to in Forsyth's writings, especially when taken along with his rendering of the sacrificial idea, which also occupies an important place in his thought, that "the sacrifice is the result of God's grace and not its cause. It is given *by* God before it is given *to* Him,"[2] that "the real meaning of an objective atonement is that God Himself made the complete sacrifice. The real objectivity of the atonement is not that it was made to God, but by God. It was atonement made by God, not by man."[3] Well, I think it must be said that Forsyth never cleared up his meaning as fully as he would have done had he written one great book on the Atonement. The emphasis on the value of Christ's holy obedience unto death, on His adequate confession of God's holiness, on His complete willingness to come within the sphere of that judgment which follows upon sin and to let that judgment break

[1] *The Cruciality of the Cross*, p. 52 f.
[2] Ibid., p. 185.
[3] *The Work of Christ*, p. 92.

over Him, takes us some way. The stress laid on the active obedience of Christ in His sufferings is certainly of great value. And Forsyth's use of the representative idea which he employed with the necessary care, while some writers are inclined to let it run away with them, helps us to understand the relationship of humanity to Christ in the Cross. This is noticeable in *The Work of Christ*. We are removed from the circle of ideas of external transactions and the like by such a passage as " whatever we mean, therefore, by substitution, it is something more than merely vicarious. It is certainly not something done over our heads. It is representative. Yet not by the will of man choosing Christ, but by the will of Christ choosing man, and freely identifying Himself with man. It is a matter not so much of substitutionary expiation (which, as these words are commonly understood, leave us too little committed), but of solidary confession and praise from amid the judgment fires, where the Son of God walks with the creative sympathy of the holy among the sinful sons of men."[1] But that in and by the Cross itself sin was judged and condemned, that there the final judgment was passed upon sin—it is certainly not easy to penetrate to the heart of these ideas which yet meant so much to Forsyth. I would suggest that anyone who desires to probe into this deep yet baffling conviction of his should read pages 81–87 and 145–148 of *The Work of Christ*, paying attention to the distinction between " although Christ was not punished by God " and " He bore God's penalty upon sin. That penalty was not lifted even when the Son of God

[1] p. 225 f.

passed through"; then he might take pages 151-155 of *The Justification of God*, and concentrate on the idea of the judgment of sin by holiness in the Cross through the conversion of "death itself from the destructive service of sin to His own redeeming service." And along with these he should read the second section of the sermon entitled, "The Fatherhood in Death" in *Missions in State and Church*,[1] where, perhaps, the view is put at its simplest and clearest— "the holiness of Christ was the one thing damnatory to the Satanic power. And it was His death which consummated that holiness. It was His death, therefore, that was Satan's fatal doom. . . . And what we call the last judgment is only the completion of the deadly judgment passed on collective evil in the Cross."

No one in modern times has penetrated nearly so far as has Forsyth into the moral reality of the Cross. And the moral reality of the Cross is the moral action of Christ on the Cross, "the Christ who Himself was driven by His experience to recognize that the crowning thing He came for was to die."[2] Forsyth was never in danger of finding himself in trouble as to the relations between the ethical and the theological. For him the theology of the Atonement meant (not only this, but certainly this) ethic at its very intensest and most commanding, while, conversely, ethic was, when traced back to its final source, theological. "The source of Christian ethic, when we go to the very root of the matter, is theological. . . . In the last radicalism it is the Cross of Christ."[3] For him the Cross was the

[1] Hodder & Stoughton, 1908.
[2] *The Cruciality of the Cross*, p. 83.
[3] *The Christian Ethic of War*, p. 85.

world's both moral and religious centre : if it was the one it could not but be the other. There he found the one real unity of the world, the teleological unity of moral purpose in " a foregone redemption, a redemption that has not now to be achieved but only actualized." [1] No one was more sure that Christ's work was a finished work. No one had a keener eye for its prolongation in the new creation of which Christ was the Head. In a sense different from and far truer than that in which the phrase is sometimes used, for Forsyth the Cross was the Eternal Cross.

III

If through His Cross, the climax of His life's work, the cup into which were poured the full riches of His moral action upon the world in God's behalf, Christ has brought real redemption and re-created humanity that in Him it may find its righteousness and its peace, the question of His Person meets us as a problem which we cannot put on one side or treat as indifferent. Soteriology passes into Christology by way, as Forsyth pointed out,[2] of soterology. Christ as Saviour is in one category ; we as saved in another. " Christ is more precious to us by what distinguishes Him from us than by what identifies Him with us." [3] Again and again Forsyth struck this note, so uncongenial to certain types of religious and even Christian thought. His longest and most elaborate antitheses are framed

[1] *The Principle of Authority*, p. 207.
[2] *The Cruciality of the Cross*, p. 25.
[3] *Hibbert Journal*, vi , April 3, 1908, " The Distinctive Thing in Christian Experience," p. 486.

THE THEOLOGY OF DR. FORSYTH

in connexion with it. One of them, opening with precisely that idea which is expressed in the last quotation, in contrast with the findings of liberal theology, fills two pages of *Positive Preaching*.[1] With Patristic theology Forsyth was not sympathetic, but his own conviction that the Christ Who so greatly saves cannot be less than God is one with the religion that was the foundation of Athanasius's theology, and he was never likely to underrate Athanasius's achievement.

Forsyth's Christology is to be studied in his Congregational Union Lecture on " The Person and Place of Jesus Christ." The book ought to be far more widely known and deeply studied than seems to be the case. Books dealing with the Christological problem in one or other of its aspects, or even surveying the whole field, are not uncommon ; but work of real greatness, work in which one feels that the writer has measured the solemn grandeur of his subject and is trying to treat of it according to its scale, is very rare. It will grow rarer if the present fancy for emphasizing, sometimes in an almost noisy manner, the Lord's humanity is allowed to have its way in theology. But apart from all contrasts, Forsyth's book is a great book. He put into it all the best of which he was capable, and the result is something equally impressive as religion and as theology. To a few of its leading ideas I will call attention, but even a long résumé would quite fail to do it justice. First, then, I would refer to his handling of the whole issue raised by the concentration upon the Synoptic Gospels, the emphasis laid upon " the

[1] pp. 327–9.

religion of Jesus," and the discovery of the essence of Christianity in the teaching of Jesus about the Fatherhood of God and about moral duty. Forsyth's argument is that it is impossible to find the secret of Christ's greatness along this line, that it does not face the full content of Christ's self-consciousness—for instance, His sense of finality, of Himself as God's final revelation, that it omits His atoning work in the Cross, and that it involves us in the conclusion that the Apostles and the Church went very far wrong, wrong with a monstrous wrongness, in their interpretation of Him, so that we have to ask, " Was Christ removed from the groping thought of Peter, Paul, and John by a greater gulf than that which parted Him from the Judaism so fatal to Him ? "[1] Secondly, the treatment of the question of Pre-existence is of great moment, and might well be pondered at a time like the present when controversy is beginning to turn on the implications of that conception. And when Forsyth thinks of Christ's pre-existence, he thinks of it in terms of the Son, and not in terms of the Logos. So did St. Paul, so did St. John, except in the prologue to the Gospel, so did the Council of Nicæa, which deliberately omitted from its Creed the word Logos, though it stood in the Creed of Eusebius, on which the conciliar creed was built. Christ was the Son, in time and also in eternity. No belief which comes short of this does justice to what Christ has meant in the experience of the Church, or to the fact that whereas " of no man can it be said that his relation to God constitutes that personality," yet " in the case

[1] p. 148.

THE THEOLOGY OF DR. FORSYTH

of Jesus the whole relation to the Father, namely, Sonship, did constitute that personality. Think it away and nothing is left."[1] Then, thirdly, the problem of the incarnate life itself is met through the application of the twin notions of kenosis and plerosis. In connexion with the former, Forsyth treads a well-beaten track, firmly but cautiously. He feels the difficulties which confront the traveller, but thinks that they are less along this route than along any other. With regard to Christ's limitations in respect of knowledge, indeed, he does not feel any difficulty. "If He did not know, it was because He consented not to know";[2] He was "by His own consent, by His emptying of Himself, limited and wrong on certain points where now, by His grace, we are right. I mean points like the authorship of a psalm, or perhaps the Parousia."[3] But where the treatment is of special interest is in respect of the relationship of Christ's manhood to the possibility of sin. Which is the true formula—*Potuit non peccare* or *Non potuit peccare?*[4] Forsyth decides for the second; but what then of the reality of the manhood? What is necessary (this is the answer) is not the possibility of sin but the possibility and reality of temptation, and as to the reality of the temptation—did Christ know that He could never fail? If He did not know, then as the temptation was real, so was the struggle against it. Forsyth writes as a man aware how great the strain upon thought, and upon more than thought, is at this point. For a moment he writes as a theologian who takes

[1] p. 285 [2] p. 317.
[3] *Hibbert Journal*, X, i., p. 245.
[4] *The Person and Place of Jesus Christ*, p. 301.

his guidance from the Chalcedonian formula might: "because Christ was true man He could be truly tempted; because He was true God He could not truly sin; but He was not less true man for that."[1] It is a question on which argument can do little for the perplexed mind. I can only say that whatever he thought of his defences, I believe that Forsyth chose the truer of two true positions. The chapter on the "Plerosis or the Self-Fulfilment of Christ" is the most original section of the book. Its importance lies in the fact that here we have a theologian, to whom the reality of Christ's Godhead is essential to Christianity, laying hold on the idea of an "acquired divinity" which has usually been held in sharp contrast to the other doctrine, and using it with most impressive effect as a true part of any complete Christology. Thus Christ "came to be what He always vitally was, by what I have called a process of moral redintegration. He moved by His history *to* a supernal world that He moved in by His nature."[2] The double movement of God to man and of man to God becomes a unity in the Person of Christ by "the mutual involution of the two personal acts or movements supreme in spiritual being, the one distinctive of man, the other distinctive of God."[3] We remember the contrast which Harnack makes in his *History of Dogma* between pneumatic and adoptionist Christology, how he points out that the dogmatic of the Church was to be based upon the former type of thought. Nicæa is as the keystone of an arch. Yet the student of doctrine who sees in the Nicene victory the triumph of the only Christo-

[1] p 302.   [2] p. 338.   [3] p 343.

logy which does justice to the implications and supports the weight of the New Testament as a whole, must allow, even with the " perfect in respect of the manhood " of Chalcedon before his eyes, that the Ancient Church paid a price for that fine and true insistence upon the reality of the Lord's Deity. The Ancient Church was not sufficiently interested in the concrete facts of His human, earthly life ; they did not mean to it what, in all reverence but in all truth, we must say, they meant to Him. Through all the great controversies up to and through the uninviting vistas of the Monophysite and Monothelite contentions, the instinct of the Church as a whole was always right. Two natures, two energies, two wills—the dogmatic decision against any one of these positions would have been a disaster. But the instinct was imperfectly applied, and Christian religion, which must live on the Christ who is human, as well as on the Christ who is divine, suffered. With all his opposition to the Liberal picture of, and theology of, Jesus, Forsyth never lost grip on the humanity of Jesus. Here are some highly significant words taken from his discussion of Holman Hunt's picture, " The Shadow of Death " : " We never can have a Christ in Art whose divinity is as unmistakable as His humanity. We have neglected and falsified the humanity in the effort to render such a Christ. Our artistic effort must now, perhaps, be rather to represent the divine Man than the human God. If Art will help us to realise the Man, if imagination will bring near us, and endear to us, and ennoble for us, the passion and presence of His human life, there are other resources which will keep us in the truth as to His Godhead." [1] That is from an earlier work of his; but its burden is theologically carried in the last chapter of his dogmatic masterpiece. It is, indeed, a very remarkable fact that Forsyth, who stood so far away from Paul of Samosata and Socinus and Unitarian theologians, did try, with all his power, to do adequate justice to that reality of the Lord's manhood on which such theologians have insisted. As one of the quotations with which Harnack prefaces the first book of the second part of his great work [2] stand words of Paul of Samosata, bearing on his view of the relation of Jesus to God, which may be thus translated: " No praise attaches to that which is attained by nature, but to that which is attained through the relationship of love high praise is due." What Paul here emphasizes, the importance of what is gained, not of what is given, is, though with no surrendering of that other vital side which Paul omits, very near to one element in Forsyth's Christology. So we have such a statement as this: " His relation to God was immediate from the first, and perfect; but that did not give Him any immunity from the moral law that we must earn our greatest legacies, and appropriate by toil and conflict our best gifts." [3] In his insistence upon the value to Christ Himself of the experiences of His human life Forsyth is in line with Du Bose. But where Forsyth presents no parallel to the American theologian is in the latter's conception of human nature in itself and of the relation of the

---

[1] *Religion in Recent Art*, p. 195.
[2] Vol III, p. 120, in the English translation.
[3] *The Person and Place of Jesus Christ*, p. 341.

THE THEOLOGY OF DR. FORSYTH

Logos to it. Forsyth would never have spoken, as Du Bose is willing to, of Jesus Christ as "the natural truth of the incarnation."[1] Anything like a speculative metaphysic of human nature was alien to him, and he distrusted the tendencies of the theology which occupied itself therewith.

It is necessary to realize, in connexion with Forsyth's Christology, that the Incarnation *in itself*, the idea of the Son of God made man, especially as presented in the Chalcedonian doctrine of the Two Natures, meant little to him. It was an idea which seemed to him to partake too much of mystic theosophy, and not to pay sufficient heed to the demands of a thoroughly ethicized religion. For him, the way to understand and to interpret the Incarnation was through soteriology. "There is the incarnation which puts us at once at the moral heart of reality—the Son made sin rather than the Word made flesh. The incarnation has no religious value but as the background of the atonement."[2] In the last book of a specifically theological character which he wrote—*The Justification of God*—there is a lengthy criticism of "Chalcedonism."[3] The word meant for him much more than a theory as to the Incarnation, but in so far as it stood for one theory, it seemed to him to depreciate the importance of God's moral action in atonement, and to lay the stress on the notion of the purification of human nature through its assumption by the Son of God. That perils beset this idea is true, also that the reduction of religious emphasis upon the Atonement, which

[1] *The Ecumenical Councils*, p. 333.
[2] *Positive Preaching*, p 182.
[3] pp 85–94

has gone along with an immense stress upon the fact of the Incarnation, possesses many unsatisfactory features. Nevertheless, Forsyth's criticism lacked proportion. The fact of the Incarnation, if fact it be, as Forsyth fully acknowledged, must have a standing and value in its own right. The contrast between "an act largely metaphysical, like the Incarnation," and "the moral Act of Atonement"[1] is not sound. And Forsyth could show, better than most, how great a moral act the Incarnation involved and was. For the Incarnation implied a great act of voluntary self-emptying, an act in which the Son anticipated all the obedience of His earthly life "in the one foregone act that brought Him to earth, the one premundane act of pregnant self-concentration for the carrying out of love's saving purpose within the world."[2] Doubtless the Incarnation looked forward to the Atonement, but an act of this kind has an ethical value of its own. Forsyth might have replied that he was only denying the value of the Incarnation in so far as that meant the juxtaposition of two natures in Christ, and the permeation of the human nature in Christ, and potentially in all men, by the virtue—semi-physically conceived—of the divine nature. But the premundane volition and its result cannot be sharply separated. If Forsyth can say of Christ's living as a finite man that "it was the greatest act of moral freedom ever done. The Godhead that freely made man was never so free as in becoming man,"[3] then the idea of the Incarnation, which arises out of the fact of the Incarna-

---

[1] *The Justification of God*, p. 91.
[2] *The Person and Place of Jesus Christ*, p. 314.   [3] Ibid., p. 315.

THE THEOLOGY OF DR. FORSYTH

tion, cannot be lacking in moral worth. There was large reason for Forsyth's reaction from much of the method in Christology which, broadly speaking, was prepared to go near to saying that incarnation itself was redemption, and reverted to the Greek patristic thought which made so much of what can happen to and in a "nature," without proper moral exigency and power of self-criticism, but I think it difficult not to admit that, at this point, Forsyth was over-much dominated by polemical necessities—true necessities, but not the only ones. Anti-Pelagian theologians (whatever form Pelagianism seems to them to be taking) ought always to be on their guard against pressing their case too far in the heat of the battle.

It is no wonder that Forsyth was little interested in the question of the Virgin Birth. It seemed to him to be of doubtful theological importance, and without relevance to the Christian experience of redemption. In *Positive Preaching* [1] he does not answer what he regards as the one theologically legitimate question with regard to it, " Was such a mode of entry into the world indispensable for Christ's work of redemption ? " It is more remarkable that, in respect of the Resurrection, he laid no stress upon the empty tomb, though he believed in it. But here too we recognize his lack of interest in physical circumstances, if only justice is done to the full moral reality of what belongs to, is a part of, God's redemptive action.[2] He was concerned not only with Christological dogma, but with its presentation according to the true order of its constituent elements. And with his own account of

[1] pp. 19–21.   [2] Ibid., pp. 255–8.

that order this section may close: "In the order of importance we should go to the world first of all with the Atoning Cross which is the Alpha and Omega of Grace; second, with the resurrection of Christ, which is the emergence into experience of the new life won for us on the Cross; third, with the life, character, teaching and miracles of Christ; fourth, with the pre-existence of Christ, which is a corollary of His Eternal Life, and only after such things with the Virgin Birth, which may or may not be demanded by the rest."[1]

IV

The distinctive and authoritative thing in Christianity was, for Forsyth, the Gospel. This, as we saw, lay, in his opinion, behind both Bible and Church as the creative power productive of both, and under the control of this primary conviction he worked out his view of what both Bible and Church meant. As to the Bible, we have gathered indications of his position. The Bible is no inerrant text-book, and the old method of handling it has broken down. It is no longer possible to make such an identification as "Revelation is the Bible which is the Word of God." The whole subject is treated at length in his article "Revelation and Bible" in the *Hibbert Journal* for October, 1911. There we have both the negative and the positive sides of his thought. And, perhaps, his meaning is best expressed if one says that he conceived of the Bible as a sacrament, and made a sharp distinction between the outward and visible sign and the inward and spiritual grace. So, to take a sentence from the article

[1] p. 128 f.

THE THEOLOGY OF DR. FORSYTH

referred to, which exhibits his conception on both of its sides, " the Bible is at once a document of man's religion and, more inwardly and deeply, a form of God's Word, and the chief form that we now have ; but as it wears a human and historic shape, it is not immune from human weakness, limitations, and error. The Bible is the great sacrament of the Word, wherein the elements may perish if only the Word itself endure."

But the Bible is not the only witness and monument of God's redeeming revelation. There is the Church as well, and one of Forsyth's most characteristic emphases is that which he is continually concerned to lay upon the Church. He could be jealous of Christian preoccupation with the thought of the Kingdom of God, when it went along with an indifference to the place and value of the Church.[1] He fought against the atomic individualism which seemed to him to be so widespread a tendency in the religion of the age, and which, when it brought in the Church at all, brought it in as a religious club or a coterie of like-minded pious people. In its grasp of the Church idea he realized and respected the strength of the Church of Rome. Great religious issues could be met only by a great Church, " and when we lose the sense of the Great Church, with its inseparable dogmatic basis, we lose the note of mastery with those commanding issues which, amid all perversion, still give such a spell to Rome."[2] For him the Church was " the Kingdom of God in the making ; "[3] or, and with the

---

[1] See *Positive Preaching*, pp. 75 ff
[2] *The Principle of Authority*, p. 258.
[3] *Theology in Church and State*, p. 209.

religious rather than the ethical interest uppermost, the Church could be interpreted through the notion of collective personality as that society, created by the Gospel, which alone is able to be, what no individual can be, " the *vis-à-vis*, and the bride, of such a universal person as Christ." [1] Hence Forsyth, when he thought of a believer's relation to Christ, thought also of the believer's position in the Church. In all salvation there was something far more than the nexus of the individual, *qua* individual, with the Saviour. Forsyth was full of the conviction (it was among his deepest) that Christ did not die for the redemption of individuals but of a race and a world, and that we do live in a redeemed world, however much has to be done towards the gathering of the fruits of that redemption. " It was a race that Christ redeemed, and not a mere bouquet of believers. It was a Church He saved, and not a certain pale of souls. Each soul is saved in a universal and corporate salvation. To be a Christian is not to attach one's salvation to a grand individual, but it is to enter Christ ; and to enter Christ is in the same act to enter the Church which is in Christ." [2]

As Forsyth exalted the idea of the Church, so did he exalt the ministry and the sacraments. Whenever he dwelt on Christian institutions, if one may use the last word in the widest sense, and so as to include the Bible, he was ready to strike the sacramental note. For instance, he asks the question : What is the meaning of an effective, a valid ministry ? and he answers : " It means sacramental. That word is my keynote. The ministry is sacramental to the Church as the

[1] *Theology in Church and State*, p. 182.
[2] *Lectures on the Church and the Sacraments*, p. 40

THE THEOLOGY OF DR. FORSYTH

Church itself is sacramental to the world," and its sacramental work lies in its conveyance of the Gospel, of which it is the "official trustee."[1] So arises his insistence on the sacramental character of preaching, and his fear lest it should be lost, for "to be effective our preaching must be sacramental. It must be an act prolonging the Great Act, mediating it, and conveying it."[2] And as he protested against any view of preaching which cut at the roots of its vital dependence upon the reverberation of and prolongation of the Gospel, so he protested against any view of Baptism and the Lord's Supper which reduced them to mere memorial rites. Whether Zwingli was a "Zwinglian" or not, we know what Zwinglianism has come to stand for, and Forsyth would have none of it. It is very noteworthy how Forsyth conceived of his differences from the Roman and from the memorial view respectively. In a number of points he differed, and differed sharply, from the former: the whole idea of infused grace acting as a regenerating substance within human nature was alien to him; he believed that it led away from the moral into the subliminal, the theosophic, and even the magical, though of this word which he used "with some protest and some reserve" he observed that "it carries associations which I do not wish to suggest, because they would be repudiated by the best of those who cherish the ideas I discard."[3] But his difference, great as it was, was not what one may call a central difference, because Forsyth penetrated behind and beneath all oppositions however deep, and reached

---

[1] *Lectures on the Church and the Sacraments*, p 125.
[2] *Positive Preaching*, p 84   [3] *Lectures*, p 207.

a deeper unity in the fact that for the believer in the Mass, as for himself, the sacrament in its inmost essence and reality meant and proclaimed the Cross, that is, the Christian Gospel. Indeed, he found this sense of the Cross in Roman rather than in Anglican Catholicism, where he found too exclusive an emphasis laid upon " the mystic participation in Christ's person without reference to moral redemption "; and " we cannot call this Catholic off-hand, for it is not the view at the central point of Catholicism—the Mass, with its Agnus Dei."[1] Now, it was this reverberation of the Gospel which he missed in the Zwinglian conception; he held " a mere memorialism to be a more fatal error than the Mass, and a far less lovely ";[2] he pleaded for a riddance " of the idea which has impoverished worship beyond measure, that the act is mainly commemoration. No Church can live on that."[3] Differently from a Roman Catholic theologian, though he construed the idea of an *opus operatum* in the Sacraments, he urged that " there is a certain place for the idea."[4] He would not allow that the Eucharist is sacrificial: " it is not the bloodless sacrifice of the Mass,"[5] and he had no place for any conception of a conveyance of grace through the elements, which were for him symbolic in the modern sense, " only as signs." Yet the emphasis he laid upon *action* in the Eucharist brought him to a point where symbolism, in the modern sense, was an inadequate account of the meaning of the Sacrament: " The action (of the Church and chiefly of Christ in the Church) is symbolic in the greater and older sense in which the symbol contains and conveys

[1] *Lectures*, p 239. [2] Ibid., p. viii [3] Ibid., p. 215.
[4] Ibid , p. 217. [5] Ibid., p. 256.

THE THEOLOGY OF DR. FORSYTH

the significate, and is a really sacramental thing. Christ offers anew to us, as He did at the supper, the finished offering which on the Cross He gave to God once for all."[1] It is, indeed, a notable fact how unwilling Forsyth was to be content with mere negations. Take the notion of mystic union with Christ through, not exclusively but particularly, sacramental communion. It was not at all congenial to him, and it would be true to say that he distrusted (I would add, often with good reason) the mystic habit of mind. But he knew that the mystic element must have its place, and to show what that place is he gave the lecture entitled " Communion—The Mystic Note." There the mystic is placed and interpreted through the moral : " the mysticism inseparable from deep religion grows moral because we are placed before the holy and not the solemn only."[2] A mysticism, whether individualistic or sacramental, which obscured the primacy of the moral and the mediation of all blessings through the Cross, came short, in his view, of the character of true religion as revealed in the New Testament. But in the union in that religion of the moral and the redemptive, and in the Christian experience which responded to it and was at home in it, he found room for the mystical element, and was far removed from the anti-mystical bias of such a theologian as Herrmann, with whom, in his emphasis upon the ethical, he had so much in common.

At the same time, with all its suggestiveness, I do not look on *Lectures on the Church and the Sacraments*

[1] *Lectures*, p. 216
[2] Ibid , p. 277. Cf. *The Principle of Authority*, p 194, " Religion is thus at bottom a moral act in a mystic sphere "

as among his very best work. Questions arise, particularly as to the Church and its ministry, which call for a more thorough-going and historical treatment than is accorded to them. For instance, if the " Great Church " is, as Forsyth certainly believed it to be, body as well as spirit, it is almost inevitable that one should want to know, " what kind of a body ? " And if the ministry has a truly sacramental character, and is the trustee of the Church's Gospel, it is surely difficult to hold that the minister receives no gift from the Church except recognition or licence, so that in ordination there is the meeting of " the authority of the Spirit in the man, and the recognition of it by the Church."[1] Forsyth was no champion of individualism at any point, no one more than he would have protested against the idea that the call to the ministry was no more than, to use his own words, " by religious sensibility," but for this very reason one desiderates an account of the relation of the Church and the ministry in which a more organic unity is discerned. And as to the Eucharist, his abandoning of, or, at least, indifference to, the idea of the Sacrament as heavenly food, which he regards as theosophic, and his method of treating the conception, stands in rather curious relation to the admission that " it is not certain that Paul did not conceive the Sacraments in a theosophic way,"[2] that " by John's time the gift (developing an element in Paul ?) had become more corporealised. The flesh of Christ replaces the body of Christ—a vivifying substance or food replaces a person in regenerating action on the moral soul,"[3] and that

[1] *Lectures*, p. 128. [2] Ibid., p. 251. [3] Ibid.

THE THEOLOGY OF DR. FORSYTH

if it helps one to think in this way, " so think, and give God thanks." [1] It is true that he has explanations to give—this aspect, if Paul held it, was not primary for him, " Paul's concepts of modality were not necessarily revelation," [2] and John when he spoke of the flesh and blood meant the personality of Jesus—but, for all that, there is something rather seriously amiss in a constructive treatment of the Eucharist which makes nothing of what is admitted as a possible element in the apostolic interpretation, and which we may presume, both on the basis of Forsyth's implications and from the very definite pages of Dr. H. T. Andrews, incorporated in the volume, in which he handles the Pauline doctrine of the sacraments from the standpoint of New Testament scholarship, to have been widespread in the apostolic Church. It is possible to be profoundly sensible of the value of Forsyth's service to institutional Christianity in the grandeur of his Church idea, in his magnifying of the ministerial office and in his exposition of the sacraments as sacraments of the Gospel, and yet to feel that he allowed his special interests to obscure the need of proportion and completeness.

V

Forsyth's independence (in the best sense of the word) and power are strikingly exhibited in his eschatology. Most theologians, when they treat of this problem, have much to say concerning the various possibilities which suggest themselves, whether from the text of the Bible or from general considerations, as to

[1] *Lectures*, p. 253.   [2] Ibid.

the destiny of man. Of this Forsyth had extraordinarily little to say. One has to catch his view from a number, not a large one, of particular hints. That he did not look on death as settling an individual's lot for ever is clear : " Its finality in the *moral* sense leads to all the enormities which we associate with the doctrine of a double predestination."[1] "We are all," he says a little later on, " predestined in love to life sooner or later, *if we will*." Yet, as we should expect, he had clearly sighted the danger in the reaction from belief in eternity of punishment, in that it " has led to dropping the idea of any hell or judgment at all, as if we could cheat judgment by dying."[2] I am not aware that he ever committed himself to universalism as an eschatological theory, though moral progress beyond the grave seemed to him certain, and "there are more conversions on the other side than on this, if the crisis of death opens the eyes as I have said."[3] Accordingly, he insisted strongly on the value of prayer for the dead : " in Christ we cannot be cut off from our dead nor they from us wherever they be. And the contact is in prayer. No converse with the dead is so much of a Christian activity as prayer for them. . . . There is nothing apostolic or evangelical that forbids prayer for them in a communion of saints which death does not rend. It is an impulse of nature which is strengthened by all we know of the movements of grace."[4]

But Forsyth's supreme interest was not in eschatology as generally construed, with its concentration

---

[1] *This Life and the Next*, Macmillan, 1918, p. 12.
[2] Ibid., p. 19   [3] Ibid., p. 42 f.   [4] Ibid, pp. 43, 49.

upon the end of human life. In an age which is continually in danger of putting man in the centre and making God the great agent for the realization of humanity's finest possibilities, he proclaimed the reality of Theodicy, of God's justification of Himself, of ends which God has set before Himself in relation to the world, and which He has already achieved and secured. Anyone who wants to probe to the bottom of Forsyth's philosophy of Christianity must take full note of this last-named and quite radical conviction of his. There is an impressive passage in *Faith, Freedom, and the Future*[1] which puts us in possession of his mind at this point : " One thing let me make clear, to avert a despotic idea of God's Lordship. It is not the Lordship of a mere imperative idealized, but of a triumphant teleology, the vast Amen. . . . Such is the moral majesty of God—God not as the Eternal Imperative of the conscience but as its everlasting Redeemer. His absolute royalty is founded in His absolute and finished salvation of the whole world. And the centre of majesty has passed, since Calvin, from the decrees of God to His Act, to the foregone establishment in Christ's Cross of a moral Kingdom without end, which is the key and goal of history." Thus the Justification of God is not something to be hoped for or expected in the future. Whatever the future holds in store, it can add nothing in principle to that moral settlement of the issues which arise between good and evil in a world of free spirits which has been made in the Cross. The theology of the Atonement is here at work on the grandest scale. " The true theology of the Cross and

[1] Hodder & Stoughton, 1912, p. 277.

its atonement is the solution of the world"; there "we have the one perfect, silent and practical confession of God's righteousness, which is the one rightness for what we have come to be, the one right attitude of the world's conscience to God's." "In His Cross, Resurrection, and Pentecost, Christ is the Son of God's love *with power*. God's love is the principle and *power* of all being. It is established in Christ everywhere, and for ever. Love so universal is also absolute and final. The world is His, whether in maelstrom or volcano, whether it sink in Beelzebub's grossness or rise to Lucifer's pride and culture. The thing is done, it is not to do." [1]

Theodicy is not a popular subject, and in so far as it is handled at all it is apt to take its shape from the supposition that things are so bad that God can be excused only if it is possible to relieve Him of responsibility. So on the one hand we are called upon to help Him as He is doing His best, on the other to find an answer to the question put in a play with a wide vogue—" And who will forgive God ? " Forsyth was always challenging this type of thought, its anthropocentrism and its lack of insight into both morals and Christianity, and especially into the meaning of the Cross. He was no expounder of a genial, sunny view of things; he was fully alive to the tragic side of life. But he found the deepest tragedy not in suffering, however poignant, but in the stricken conscience and the fettered will. Among the moderns he found his prophets in such names as Carlyle and Ibsen and Wagner and Kierkegarde. But he believed that the worst devilries were

[1] *The Justification of God*, pp. 125, 174, 171 f.

THE THEOLOGY OF DR. FORSYTH 107

already smitten with a mortal blow, so that, though they lived on in the world, the world was for ever beyond their capture and control; for God " has the evil, even of such a world as we see, in the hollow of His hand. That is the Christian faith. If His holy way spared not His own Son, i.e. His own Self, that holiness is secured finally for the whole world, with its most cynical immorality, deadly malignity, and cruel frightfulness." [1]

Theodicy means the certainty of the Kingdom of God. The idea of the Kingdom does not hold so obviously prominent a place in Forsyth's writings as it does in a good deal of modern theology. Nevertheless, it emerges in power, especially in connexion with the social and historical implications of the Gospel. And he has much to say about it in his later works, in *The Justification of God*, *The Christian Ethic of War*, and *This Life and the Next*, all written in the stress of the war. The judgment which he saw descending upon civilization in the war he regarded as the inevitable penalty for the neglect of the Kingdom.[2] And the service of the Kingdom is no merely individual obligation, but " men in nations must serve the Kingdom, and not merely as individuals, groups, or Churches; for a nation has a personality of its own," and even war could be " an agent of His Kingdom," [3] which is " the emergence into the life of history, both by growth and crisis, of that saving sovereignty which is the moral power and order of the spiritual world.

[1] *The Justification of God*, p 154.
[2] Ibid., p 104.
[3] *The Christian Ethic of War*, p. 189.

The coming of the Kingdom is the growth or the inroad of God's Will on earth to be what it always is in peace and glory in Heaven," and " only in the active love and service, not simply of God, but of the Kingdom of God and His Christ, are the full powers of the soul released and its resources plumbed. The Kingdom of God is only another phrase for the energetic fullness of man's eternal life—here or hereafter." [1] But the Kingdom, whose establishment and victory is the concrete manifestation of theodicy, is not essentially a reality round which the hopes and aspirations and endeavours of men may gather : it is already present, won, and secured, in the Cross. For Christ was no martyr, even though the greatest, but He " went to the Cross as King of the world," and the Cross " is not only very real but fontal, creative and final for the Kingdom of God to which all history moves. . . . The Cross enacts on an eternal scale the moral principle which is subduing all history at last to itself and its holy love. The judgment *process* in history only unfolds the finality of the Eternal judgment *act* which is in the Cross, to recondense it in the final settlement of all things." [2] By no theologian of our age has a deeper-rooted optimism been expressed.

I have tried to bring into view those elements in Forsyth's theology on which he himself was accustomed to lay the greatest stress. But I am conscious of much which has been omitted for which a place, in any full treatment of that theology, would have to

[1] *This Life and the Next*, pp 85, 92.
[2] *The Justification of God*, pp 154, 189.

THE THEOLOGY OF DR. FORSYTH

be found—the relationship between holiness and love, the reality of holiness within the Godhead as Holy Spirit leading on to the doctrine of the Trinity, the state of man as involving not merely tragic accidents but universal guilt, the interweaving of Christianity's redemption-motive with great art and great politics. Yet this may be said here : the student who cares to trace out Forsyth's thought on any one of these great matters will find that everything moves round one centre, reverts to one principle, rests on one bed-rock. There is a true sense in which Forsyth was a man of one idea—the Cross. But that idea, or rather act and fact, was for him so universal and eternal, all-compassing, all-penetrating, all-absorbing, that he was able to combine a great simplicity with a great subtlety and richness, which, if regarded merely as a *tour de force*, is amazing. To go abroad, as it has been necessary to do, in the wide fields of his writings, has been to grow still more impressed with the extraordinary fertility and richness of his thought It is great theology, the theology of one as scientifically competent as Ritschl, as spiritually proficient as Dale. And through it all burns the passion of one inspired by a single motive—the greater glory of God, his Redeemer.

IV

THE WORK OF CHRIST IN MODERN THEOLOGY

THE number of important books dealing with the doctrine of the Atonement from the point of view of historical exposition or constructive treatment, and, in more than one case, combining history and theory so as to bring out more fully the character of the writer's theology, has been a remarkable feature of British work in the field of Christian doctrine during recent years. It is something of a surprise: on the whole, the tendency of theological interest in the present century had been in the direction of the meaning of the Kingdom of God and of the fact and implications of the Incarnation. Nor had the trend of religious emphasis corrected this movement. In the Church of England, one great section of opinion laid the stress and weight of its appeal upon the Sacraments; another still maintained a certain undogmatic tradition and spirit which was more at home with the proclamation of the Fatherhood of God and the moral excellence of the teaching of Christ than with a systematized theology. And the latter standpoint had considerable support within English Nonconformity. There was a general reaction from the old-time concentrated emphasis upon soteriology.

The hard, stark objectivity of the expiatory doctrine which had been the classical form in which the Protestant theologians had interpreted and expressed the idea of atonement seemed less ethically tolerable ; there was a prevalent consciousness of the difficulty of isolating the work of Christ in His death from His life's work as a whole, and of the need for an appreciation of the Person of Christ which should give the notion of incarnation a standing in its own right, and not subordinate it to the passive endurance of suffering upon the Cross. To some extent this need merely reproduced the sense which the Protestant scholastics had of the necessity for finding a place for Christ's active, as well as for His passive, obedience ; but the whole atmosphere was different from that in which Piscator and Gerhard, as quoted by Mr. Grensted in a book to which I shall refer more fully, could argue as to where the redemptive value of Christ's work was to be found. At the Universities there was the same story to tell : Westcott's powerful influence, his profound sense of the riches hid in the Person of Christ, of a gospel of creation resumed in the Incarnation and perfected in the Resurrection, inevitably reduced the significance of the death of Christ as a solitary saving act ; while, at Oxford, the Lux Mundi school, though its starting-point was not Westcott's (it was dogmatic and ecclesiastical, he biblical and speculative), nor its interests and aims the same, tended to find Christianity's religious and theological centre in the Incarnation itself, in " the taking of the manhood into God." One of the greatest of modern treatises on soteriology, *Atonement and Personality*, came from a member of this school, and nowhere has its most radical and characteristic conceptions been more thoroughly worked out. It marked an epoch; it revived interest in soteriology; all more recent developments come to a settlement with it in one way or other; but it was far from being a return to earlier views. It is quite true that Dr. Moberly goes back beyond Anselm to the Fathers, and finds help in Clement of Rome, Irenæus, and Athanasius, but for all that his construction is not a revival of patristic theology, but, at most, of one element which was never held in isolation.

Without exaggerating the extent of the change, a change there has been. The insistence on the Cross as the end of His ministry, regarded by Christ as inevitable, which was one feature in the eschatological reaction from the old liberal reading of the Gospels, had some effect; the continual urging of the expiatory element as the essential thing in the Cross, in a never-tiring stream of books and articles from about the years 1905 onwards, from the pen of Dr. Forsyth, was too remarkable—both provocative and stimulating—in character not to exercise a wide and strong influence; and the break with historic Christianity which could not be overlooked in certain restatements, which showed the working of the general liberal tradition, perhaps recalled more conservative theology and more classical piety to an appreciation of the relevance of the fact that the Cross, and nothing else, was the distinctive symbol of the Christian religion, that it was not sufficient to concentrate attention on Christ's Person and neglect His work. The Socinian controversy had a lesson here for those who knew the facts. In any case, while it is difficult to analyze adequately the causes and processes of the movement, there resulted a change in the balances and proportions of theological emphasis.

It may be asked whether the war has had its share in speeding this tendency. To some extent one may answer "Yes"; but in respect of aspects of the subject, rather than of the whole subject. The war compelled attention to the problem of the character of God's sympathy with the sufferings of man, and to the problem of theodicy—of the justification of God. Both these problems are vitally connected with the death of Christ, but whereas in the first of the two the naturalness of the connexion (granted the Catholic doctrine of Christ's Person) does not lead directly to a doctrine of atonement, in the second the vital connexion is not immediately obvious; the referring of the justification of God to the Cross of Christ as to its one proper *locus revelationis* is a very striking instance of Dr. Forsyth's theological insight and power of subtle combination. More generally the war raised in an acute form the question of the whole character of Christian ethic, and any settlement reached or tendencies manifested with regard to this must, in the long run, affect the doctrine of the Atonement.

It is within the last four or five years that so much important work on the Atonement has been published; to it I wish now to turn. One series of articles, lately published, I have not read, except to a very small extent, and therefore must pass by. I refer to Dr.

Robert Mackintosh's contributions to the *Expositor* ;[1] otherwise, I hope that nothing of the first importance is being overlooked. What is particularly interesting about the work in question is that it is representative of widely divergent, and of mediating, points of view ; a survey of it will help us to see how widely is still being manifested the result of the fact that, as Dr. Headlam said in his inaugural lecture at Oxford, " there is no Catholic explanation of the Atonement."

The first book which I wish to mention is the volume of Moorhouse Lectures, published in 1916 by Canon Hart of St. Paul's Cathedral, Melbourne, under the title *Spiritual Sacrifice*.[2] Canon Hart is concerned with the exploration and elucidation of the true character of worship, and, in particular, with the Eucharist. To that end he deals first with theories of sacrifice and atonement, and develops an attack upon the Western doctrine " of a meritorious self-sacrifice, placating or satisfying God by its intrinsic value." He rejects the whole idea of a reparation made by Christ as man. But the interesting point about Canon Hart's own view is that he does not relapse into Abelardian conceptions, but claims that his own view is the least subjective one possible, since the Atonement is for him a wholly divine work, effected by Christ when He was made man completely—not in Bethlehem, but on Calvary. Thus there is a resemblance—Canon

[1] Since writing this article in *Theology* I reviewed Dr Mackintosh's book, *Historic Theories of Atonement, with Comments*, Hodder & Stoughton, 1920, in the *Journal of Theological Studies* (April, 1922). Few treatises on the subject are so readable, but it is concerned with criticism rather than construction

[2] *Spiritual Sacrifice*, by John Stephen Hart, M A , B Sc (Longmans. 1916) 4s. 6d. net.

Hart would say more—to that patristic view, notably present in Irenæus and Athanasius, which expresses itself in such a statement as " He was made man that we might be made divine." Canon Hart's position is not a little difficult of apprehension, because whereas, on the one hand, Christ's sacrifice is found to consist in His identification with human sin, no idea of expiation is allowed a place. There was nothing more to do when on the Cross, and finally by dying, Christ was made " very man." It is plain enough that this is a work altogether objective, altogether God's. But, at the same time, we come back, full circle, to one of the chief characteristics of all subjective views—that satisfaction and propitiation Godwards are ideas which have no place in a true doctrine of atonement. What is it that Christ does? is the decisive soteriological question. It is the question concerning not the Author of our salvation, that He was God, essential though this confession is, but the work which for our salvation He wrought. And in the answer to this lies, as I believe, the fundamental strength of the Western tradition.

This tradition is very lucidly exemplified in a quotation from another volume of the year 1916: Dr. Sparrow Simpson's *Reconciliation between God and Man*.[1] He sums up the doctrine of reparation, which seems to him, unlike Canon Hart, an essential element in atonement, as follows: " Christ is God's greatest Gift to man. And when the Father gave us Christ, He furnished humanity with the means of making its

---

[1] *Reconciliation between God and Man*, by W. J Sparrow Simpson, D.D. (S P.C.K. 1916) 3s net

own Godward reparation." The essence of this reparation is expressed in a way that recalls both McLeod Campbell and Moberly: in Christ the Father heard a new thing, "a human voice pronouncing perfect judgment on human sin; perfectly concurring in the judgment of the Father upon sin; gathering up, and fusing into one, and perfecting, all the earth's imperfect reparations; and offering a perfect sorrow for the sin of the world." Here is something very different in its notion of the situation created by sin, and of the need for a treatment of that settlement, from the bold conclusion which Canon Hart draws out as the results lying behind the theory of a ransom to Satan —" What did God do because of man's sin? In a very true sense He did nothing. He continued to carry out the purpose with which He had made the worlds." Only that purpose of union effected between man and God now meant that " the Son of God took to Himself the race of men—took us with our sin." I cannot but think that at this point Canon Hart is nearer to certain philosophical conceptions of the relationship between God and the world's evil than to the New Testament. One may not be content with Dr. Sparrow Simpson's emphasis upon the reparation made by humanity, and may be surprised at the confidence with which he can say that had Christ died a peaceful death at home " He would none the less have redeemed the world " (would there then have been the same strain on that obedience of His will which is the great internal action of the Cross ?), but the substance of his thought has that Pauline quality which again and again—though it would not be fair

CHRIST IN MODERN THEOLOGY

to bring Canon Hart's volume into the comparison—makes the crucial difference between a theology at once evangelical and catholic and theological liberalism.

The year 1917 saw the issue of one notable work on soteriology, Dr. Denney's *The Christian Doctrine of Reconciliation*.[1] Published after its author's death, it was a final offering to that truth which had been the most luminous and powerfully creative fact in his experience. There was a hardness about the grain of Dr. Denney's mind which it is impossible not to regret; he was not widely sympathetic, and he could be a drastically severe critic. But the presence of this element in his writings on the Atonement testified to his profound sense of the greatness of the work Christ had done, of all that it meant to him as a Christian believer, and of the need for a watchful jealousy, lest that which was the very centre and secret of the power of Christ's saving work should be hidden away or minimized in restatements of the doctrine.

His last volume is, however, so far as the first five chapters are concerned, more conciliatory in tone than any work of his with which I am acquainted. It is unfortunate that in the final chapter there is a reversion to the less pleasing characteristics of his temper. The fact is that Dr. Denney was extraordinarily out of sympathy with typical Catholic piety. The Incarnation, construed as "the taking up of human nature into union with a divine person," meant, it is fair to say, nothing to him at all. The whole theology of Christ's natures was alien to him. He says outright

[1] *The Christian Doctrine of Reconciliation*, by James Denney, D.D. (Hodder & Stoughton. 1917.) 7s. 6d. net.

that the only thing he can understand by the Incarnation is "the actual historical life and death of Christ." He had no philosophy of the union of God and man in Christ, and did not feel the need of any; that is part of the fact that, as Dr. H. R. Mackintosh said of him, in an illuminating notice in the *Expository Times*, he had never settled accounts with philosophy. Inevitably, when he handles mysticism or the Sacraments, he reveals almost the dourest kind of Protestant reaction from every sort of conception of infused grace: he even thinks it desirable to say that the terms "consecrated or unconsecrated," used of the eucharistic elements, are "expressions totally destitute of New Testament authority"—all of which only goes to show that Dr. Denney's limitations, like all his other qualities, were strongly marked.

There is more of an historical survey in this volume than in earlier ones devoted to the doctrine of the Atonement. Broadly speaking, it shows that no particular system, neither Anselm's satisfaction theory, nor the Reformers' teaching of penal substitution, fully satisfied Dr. Denney. That thoroughgoing high Calvinist, Dr. B. B. Warfield, in his review of this book in the *Princeton Theological Review*, noted with regret a continuation of a tendency to Grotian theories (Christ's death as a penal example, but not rigorously demanded by the righteousness of God) which he had previously observed in Dr. Denney: he missed the outspoken

> In my place condemned He stood,
> Hallelujah!

It would probably be true to say that Dr. Denney grew less willing to affirm the theory of penal substitution in any precise formula. What one notices with great satisfaction in *The Christian Doctrine of Reconciliation* is the emphasis laid upon love. We might think that it was the exponent of a very different type of doctrine who speaks in such sentences as " Love proved itself in the Passion of Jesus to be the final reality, and no truth which takes possession of the heart of man can ever have power to subdue and reconcile like this " ; or, of the demerits of Anselm's theory, " Perhaps the most conspicuous is that Anselm gives no prominence to the love of God as the source of the satisfaction for sin, or to the appeal which that love makes to the heart of sinful men " ; or, and very strikingly, " The life of Jesus, from beginning to end, is in all its relations to others a life of love. It is love, then, we have to understand." The older theologians, in the line of descent from whom Dr. Denney has his place, would hardly have denied the truth of such utterances ; but they would hardly have spoken in this way themselves. And most striking is his refusal to distinguish in justification between a *fides informis* and a *fides caritate formata*. A very real bridge is built between Catholic and Protestant conceptions, when the faith which unites the Christian with Christ is a faith " to which love is integral, because it is itself a response to a love which passes knowledge."

It must not be imagined that Dr. Denney has withdrawn in any way from his grasp of the objectivity, the Godward bearing, of the Atonement. He is convinced of the truth of the retributive view of punishment expressed in the fact of " the inevitable reactions of the divine order against evil." He will not surrender such words as "propitiation," "expiation," "substitution." His view of the New Testament perspective has not altered. But I think that a reader cherishing a different doctrine of the work of Christ would feel the atmosphere of the first five chapters less alien, and, one may perhaps say, less forbidding than *The Death of Christ*, and even *The Atonement and the Modern Mind*. Those who, like Canon Storr, were conscious of a profound debt to Dr. Denney for the first of these two earlier works, will feel that by this last volume that debt is increased.

Canon Storr's *The Problem of the Cross* (1919)[1] is an expansion of lectures. It is thorough, without being technical. I doubt whether there exists any better book for putting into the hands of an inquirer who feels difficulties about the Atonement. Canon Storr is a philosopher, and there is some excuse for distrusting philosophers when they handle that great doctrine; there is the danger of something like a μετάβασις εἰς ἄλλο γένος. But Canon Storr's approach to the subject has two great merits—he gives full weight to the New Testament teaching, and he emphasizes the reality of the moral order of the universe and the need for some reparation to it, since it has been violated by sin. With regard to this last point a word of comment may be in place. Here we are in the presence of one of the great dividing-lines in soteriological theory. It is impossible to prove that reparation for the violation of the moral order is necessary. It is, I believe, an ultimate deliverance of

[1] *The Problem of the Cross*, by Vernon F. Storr, M.A. (John Murray. 1919.) 5s. net.

CHRIST IN MODERN THEOLOGY

conscience, and can be neither analyzed, demonstrated, nor refuted. The Christian conscience has, on the whole, tended to affirm the need, and still tends to affirm it. Canon Storr does not shrink from allowing a penal element in the Cross: Christ " entered into the doom of sin. He underwent what sin entails in the race "; and, with the idea of satisfaction rather than of penalty uppermost, " by His death Christ paid homage to the sanctity of the moral order." Canon Storr does not find the whole truth of the Atonement in such ideas; he accepts, following Moberly in linking together Calvary and Pentecost, a form of the representative theory; he accepts the " moral influence " theory as true, though not the whole truth, and makes the good point that the positive element in this theory is included in the substitutionary and representative theories when these are rightly expounded, which is, in effect, what we saw to be the case in Dr. Denney's emphasis on love. Finally, Canon Storr is specially suggestive in his extremely careful treatment of the subject of " the suffering God," and his interpretation of that idea through the Cross. It is, I am sure, only by our understanding of the Person and Passion of Christ that we can hope to understand the truth that there is in the notion of the suffering of God.

On a bigger scale than *The Problem of the Cross* is Mr. Snowden's *The Atonement and Ourselves*,[1] a book which shows that it may still be the proud and justifiable boast of the Church of England that it is not

---

[1] *The Atonement and Ourselves*, by P. L. Snowden. (S.P.C.K 1919.) 10s. 6d. net.

only to the Universities and to theologians in the narrower sense of the word that she has to look for good theology. There are two main thoughts which Mr. Snowden develops: the first shows him to be at one with Dr. Denney and Canon Storr in emphasizing the reality of the moral order of the universe, the necessity of reparation for sin, and the place of a penal element in the Cross. Indeed, Mr. Snowden goes beyond Dr. Denney in his emphasis upon the requirements which result from the nature of God. Dr. Denney has more to say of God's love than of God's holiness, though for him that love does not in the least render the whole substitutionary and penal view invalid, an assumption not uncommon among liberal theologians. Mr. Snowden deliberately subordinates love to holiness when he thinks of the Divine nature. Holiness is basal; love is a supreme quality: "though holiness is necessary to the very existence of love, love is only necessary to the completeness of holiness." One might be reading a lucid commentary on some characteristic passage of Dr. Forsyth's. And much as I sympathize with what is at the back of writing of this kind, I do not like what treats as a possible reality a God holy but not loving. Mr. Snowden is quite definite: "Holiness can exist as truth, purity, justice, etc., without love." But whether this is abstractly conceivable or not, I object to any argument with regard to the God revealed in Christ being founded upon it; for there is nothing whatever to sanction the idea of a possible separation between holiness and love in that God.

The first main division of the book is, then, a con-

CHRIST IN MODERN THEOLOGY 123

sidered argument for the need of an objective atonement, and for the fact of that atonement in the Passion of Jesus Christ, Who, while He did not endure punishment, yet endured suffering, which in itself possessed a penal quality. Mr. Snowden sides with Dale as against McLeod Campbell, Moberly, and others in refusing to put upon the cry from the Cross, " My God, My God, why hast Thou forsaken Me ? " any other interpretation than that Christ did submit " to the awful suffering arising from ' the loss of the sense of God's presence.' " Certainly, if Mr. Snowden had laid down his pen at the end of Chapter III of Part IV, no one could have had any real reason to doubt that he had affirmed, clearly and uncompromisingly, a doctrine of the Atonement derived, with practically no intrusion of alien elements, from the Reformers rather than from Anselm.

But with the second main division there comes a change. In one sense it seems a wholly legitimate change, for however objective the Atonement be, and, indeed, the more objective it is, the greater becomes the necessity for the expression of an intelligible relationship between Christ's work and ourselves. This was what Dr. Moberly felt so acutely: the Atonement must be vitalizing in man, and the key to this lay in Rom. viii, whereas Dr. Dale appeared to him to have stopped with Rom. vii. Nor was Dr. Denney unconscious of the need ; all that he puts into the idea of faith, that " passion in which the whole being of man is caught up and abandoned unconditionally to the love revealed in the Saviour," is proof. But where Mr. Snowden's change ceases to be quite legitimate is in the use he makes of the thought, to which he devotes great attention, of the identification of the Christian with Christ. One begins to realize that one is on a different road in the section headed *Christ's Crucifixion was only a Potential Atonement to be completed by and in each Believer*; there we learn that " only . . . the means were then [by our Lord's death] provided for atonement "; we are away from actual completed reparation; the reality has yet to come. The necessary *prius* to this is the identification of the Christian with Christ, the Incarnation is extended through a oneness effected between individuals and our Lord " by means of a union with Him as nearly identical in nature to this [the Incarnation] as possible," whereunto is directed the power of the Holy Ghost operating through the Sacraments. And so, because of the life of Christ in the Christian, and because the past fact of His crucifixion lives on in the Christian's present life, involving a real connexion between the Christian and the sacrifice of Calvary, to which, moreover, the moral character of his life bears witness, Mr. Snowden comes to a conclusion as definite as, but how different from, any conclusion in the former main division : " It becomes clear it is not the suffering of the innocent, but of the guilty—not of Christ, but ourselves—which satisfies the claims of justice."

Now one need not share Dr. Denney's dislike of the phrase " mystical union," and of the ideas usually connoted thereby, to be convinced that a doctrine of identification amounting to the *unio mystica*, which leads anyone—and especially the writer of pages 1 to 189 of *The Atonement and Ourselves*—to frame a sentence like the above, wants resetting. The union of the Christian with Christ, interpret it as you will, and supplementing Dr. Denney's conception with something more mystical, is, in the New Testament, always the fruit of Calvary, and is related to Calvary in no other way whatsoever. When St. Paul said, " I am crucified with Christ," he did not mean that he had any share in Christ's work upon the Cross; immediately afterwards he speaks of the Son of God " who loved me and gave Himself for me," the logical *prius* to that experience which could be described as Christ living in him. It is perfectly true that the Christian's union is with the whole Christ, the Christ Who has been crucified, not simply the Christ Who now lives in glory, but that union does not involve such an interchange of characteristics between Christ and the Christian, or Christ and the whole Church, as would make of the Christian or the Church both Redeemer and redeemed.

It is impossible not to regret the second main division of Mr. Snowden's book. The author had a great purpose in view; after establishing the necessity for objective atonement, and keeping close to the New Testament in his exposition of the sufferings of Christ, he desired to show that an intelligible relationship between Calvary and the new Christian life could be expressed. Unfortunately, he allowed, what Dr. Denney never allows, his grasp of what he already held to slacken; he left his moorings and went off into mysticism and speculation, into analogies psychological and sociological, without any proper biblical and moral control. The fault is a serious one, and it was not in any way inevitable. If I feel compelled to lay stress upon it, it is because there is so much that is strong and good in Mr. Snowden's book, and if only it had developed to the end on right lines it would have been a really notable piece of work.

Something must now be said on the two historical surveys, Principal Franks' very full record in two volumes, entitled, *A History of the Doctrine of the Work of Christ*,[1] and Mr. Grensted's *A Short History of the Doctrine of the Atonement* (1920).[2] In its thoroughness, Principal Franks' work in this particular field is comparable to Rivière's *Essai de l'Etude historique*—and the Englishman covers more ground; but the real comparison is with one of those massive German works which delight in showing how, beneath the surface of the history, certain principles or fundamental dogmatic impulses are at work, leading to particular constructions and syntheses, which are destined to lose their solidity under the solvent action of other powerful forces which work towards new crystallizations. There is something of Harnack about the book, and something of Ritschl: it is considerably more than a record of successive doctrines of the Atonement; what is meant to appear at the various points of critical summing-up is the expression of a whole concept of Christianity in a dominant view of Christ's work. Where that concept cannot, in the author's opinion, be gathered simply from the formal doctrine of the work of Christ, he finds it necessary, for the sake of completeness, to expand his outlook

---

[1] *A History of the Doctrine of the Work of Christ*, by Robert S. Franks, M A , B Litt 2 vols (Hodder & Stoughton) 18s.

[2] *A Short History of the Doctrine of the Atonement*, by L W. Grensted, M A , B D. (Longmans, Green & Co., Publishers to the Manchester University Press 1920) 9s. 6d.

CHRIST IN MODERN THEOLOGY

so as to include doctrines of law and of the Sacraments. This is the case with the Western mediæval dogmatic. The treatise is not easy reading, but there is a great deal in it which an English reader will look in vain for elsewhere. Mr. Grensted's *Short History* is less formidable. It is a straightforward account, with ample quotations, of the progress of thought on the Atonement. Constructive it is not intended to be, but no one (unless Principal Franks is an exception) can write a history of this doctrine without showing, more or less clearly, where he himself stands. Mr. Grensted holds to the objective theory in its satisfactionary form, with the influence of Moberly admitted but not obtruded. He is favourable to mystical conceptions of the union of the believer with Christ, but it is clear that he would be far more cautious and reserved in speculation than Mr. Snowden, far less likely ever to mix up different stages in the objective work and the response to it. It is not a book that will help revolutionary spirits—which is not, in my opinion, a condemnation of it.

Note —In fairness to Mr Snowden, I must call attention to the fact that in a communication to the Editor of *Theology*, mentioned in vol 1, No 6 (December, 1920), of that journal he " asks to be allowed to disclaim any views which, from Mr Mozley's review, might be attributed to him to the effect : (1) that separation is possible between the holiness and love of God; (2) that the Christian is both Redeemer and redeemed , (3) that our Lord's sacrifice for sin is not complete as a full, perfect, and sufficient satisfaction for the sins of the whole world " And I am glad also to refer to Mr. Snowden's very definite defence of the objective character of the Atonement as set forth in his articles on "Dr Rashdall's Theory of the Atonement " in *Theology*, vol 11, Nos 19 and 20 (January and February 1922)

V

DR. RASHDALL ON THE ATONEMENT

DR. RASHDALL's Bampton Lectures, *The Idea of Atonement in Christian Theology*, were delivered in 1915 and published in 1919.[1]

Here is a work which, for many a day to come, will be appealed to by the English supporters of the subjective interpretation; " Rashdall " will be named in the same sort of way as " Dale " and " Moberly." If you do not like it you must recognize its power; it is on the big scale which befits the subject; it is written in a spirit of extraordinary confidence, with practically no reservations (none at points of first-rate importance), as though the author were confident that the time had come to have done with the English caution which is glad not to dispense altogether with anything, and to say boldly that there is one true doctrine of the Atonement, and one only, and that is Abelard's. Dr. Rashdall is as rigorous as Dr. Denney; the latter was exceedingly impatient of people who seemed not to know their way about the classic paths of Christian experience; the former conveys the impression of almost equal impatience with those who

[1] *The Idea of Atonement in Christian Theology*, by Hastings Rashdall, D.Litt., D.C.L., LL D., Dean of Carlisle. (Macmillan. 1919.) 15s. net.

seem to him to be strangers to the high work of true thinking. It is a tragic thing that we shall not read Dr. Denney's review of Dr. Rashdall, and any reply to which the latter might have felt called. Yet in one important respect there is real similarity between the two: neither is friendly towards the kind of mystical conception of Christ's human nature which not uncommonly emerges in connexion with the "representative" doctrine; both are decisively opposed to Moberly in what was to that theologian a matter of fundamental importance; "a pretentious and not very intelligible idea of Christ's metaphysical relation to mankind" is Dr. Denney's estimate of the notion of Christ's inclusive humanity; Dr. Rashdall is equally severe: "as to the theory that Christ is Himself 'the universal of humanity' and not merely a particular man, that is surely a form of words to which no intelligible meaning can be attached." It is important to observe that his Christology is here in closest connexion with his soteriology. He will not allow that Christ's humanity was "impersonal"; as I understand him, the enhypostasia doctrine of Leontius of Byzantium would not satisfy him, since for him Jesus Christ is *a particular man* (my italics), in whose human life and character God uniquely revealed Himself by a complete union between the logos of God and Christ's human soul. It is the old Antiochene tradition with regard to Christ's Person pushed very far, and in these pages of Dr. Rashdall I feel what other writings of his have made me feel—the desire that he should show how or whether, if his Christological and Trinitarian conceptions (the doctrine of a particular man completely united with the Logos, and of the Trinity as One Mind which admits of no distinction of thought and consciousness as between the Father, the Son, and the Holy Spirit) are, as he certainly would maintain, Catholic, there is any real division between Catholic doctrine and Unitarianism —not necessarily in its early Socinian form, but in statements about God and Christ which would accept the conception of God as Power, Wisdom, and Will or Love, and allow of a special relationship between Jesus and God. Where is the dividing-line ? " That God is Power, and Wisdom, and Love is simply the essence of Christian Theism—not the less true because few Unitarians would repudiate it " : these are Dr. Rashdall's words in an earlier book, *Philosophy and Religion*. Is, then, the Unitarian controversy intellectually dead ?

This digression, while far from unimportant in itself, makes it appear only natural that Dr. Rashdall should give up the whole substitutionary conception, in whatever form it is held. The substitution of Jesus, a particular of humanity, for all other particulars, is neither rationally nor morally defensible. I have referred to Dr. Rashdall's position as Antiochene : it is interesting to note how, in his confession of faith, given in Hahn's *Bibliothek* (3rd edition, pp. 302-304), Theodore of Mopsuestia, the great Antiochene theologian, when he mentions Christ's saving work, expresses it as " the leading of all " by Christ, the Lord from heaven, " to imitate Himself " ; later on he speaks of " the saving repentance." The former idea is not far removed from that emphasis which Dr. Rashdall lays upon the words of Christ, and the moral ideal embodied in His teaching and character

In Dr. Rashdall's argument we may note the following important positions and conclusions. Firstly, there is nothing in the Gospels, properly interpreted, which sharply distinguishes the character of Christ's work on the Cross from the work of His whole ministry, nor is any doctrine of expiatory sacrifice to be extracted from the Ransom passage, or from Christ's words at the Last Supper. Where there is sincere human repentance, there is bestowed the divine forgiveness, is the doctrine of our Lord. Secondly, the Early Church found a prophecy of Christ's death in Isaiah liii, and applied to Him the conceptions of a sin-bearing sufferer which that chapter of Scripture contains ; except in the case of St. Paul, no theory was devised, the Church rested on traditional formulas ; St. Paul, under pressure of the controversy about the law, presented the death of Christ as an expiation for the sins of men ; he did not work out an entirely clear theory of substituted sacrifice or substituted punishment, but the idea cannot be evaded ; and in this he stood alone. Thirdly, the most spiritual patristic view of the Atonement is to be found among Eastern, not Western, Fathers, the ethic of the latter being deeply harmed by the legalism inherent in it ; of Tertullian and Augustine Dr. Rashdall is a severe critic. Fourthly, the Anselmic doctrine of satisfaction, which, in a modified form, was incorporated in the Thomist theology, is not to be essentially distinguished from the penal theology of the Reformers ; but the scholastics had a definite advantage in their view of justification as a making just, which, though philologically untenable, contains a far more adequate idea than the forensic interpretation, to which Luther clung so passionately. Though it is not at the centre of Dr. Rashdall's work, few things in the book are more interesting than his treatment of this controversy. And one may say that at this point he is certainly clearer than Dr. Denney. I have already shown how for the Scottish theologian *fides* is essentially not *informis*, but *caritate formata*. " Trust and love," he says, " are indissolubly intertwined " : yet he praises Luther for his emphasis on faith alone ; it is true that he goes on to add that every Christian experience, call it sanctification or love or regeneration, " lies within faith and is dependent upon it." But is this what Luther meant ? Dr. Rashdall interprets him very differently ; that for Luther faith is simply belief, and that salvation by faith only meant for the Reformer " salvation by faith without love." Yet Dr. Rashdall admits another strain, in which faith is identified with confidence or trust. In so far as the question is a really living one, a concordat ought not to be impossible. Fifthly, the expiatory view implies the retributive view of punishment, a view whose ancestry Dr. Rashdall finds in the primitive desire for revenge, and which he judges to be inconsistent with God's character as love.

All of these points raise great issues, and with some of them I have dealt in a review for another journal. Here I would concentrate criticism in two or three remarks. Firstly, Dr. Rashdall's treatment of the New Testament seems more impressive than sound ;

DR. RASHDALL ON THE ATONEMENT 133

he has said what can be said against the view that Christ connected His death with the forgiveness of sins, without nearly reaching the point where the defenders of a position must feel that they are fighting a losing battle against an overwhelming weight of argument. He presses, further than the evidence warrants, the idea that the New Testament writers, other than St. Paul, used, as to the objective efficacy of Christ's death, traditional formulæ which—so I judge the argument to run—bore no relation to any spiritual experience which they possessed. And no slight problem seems to be raised if, in his doctrine of the substitutionary Atonement, St. Paul was as wrong—intellectually and morally—as on Dr. Rashdall's view we must (whatever allowances we make for the age in which he lived, and special facts of his temperament) regard him. The objective atonement was not the whole of St. Paul's Gospel, but it was integral to it, and even at its centre; if St. Paul was wrong at this point, then 1 Cor. ii, the classic chapter on apostolic inspiration, needs rewriting.

Secondly, Dr. Rashdall's pages seem to reflect neither the New Testament nor the Christian conscience, as seen in the great saints and in the normal attitude of Christian believers, in respect of God's holiness, human sin, and the reaction of the former from the latter. The doctrine of objective atonement rests upon the conviction of the disintegration of the moral order—so far as that is possible—caused by man's sin, and of the necessity of some great act—call it reparation, satisfaction, penalty, confession—whereby the wrong done to that moral order shall be put right.

For Dr. Rashdall the whole matter is simply on the individualistic level: one man, and another, and so on, sins and repents, and there is the Atonement, inasmuch as to that repentance nothing so certainly contributes as the sight of Christ crucified. The Atonement is more of a process than an act on this showing; the death of Christ, the awakening of love and repentance, the moral improvement all belong to it. It is this individualistic outlook which is challenged by such ideas as those of corporate guilt or a guilty humanity to which Dr. Rashdall objects. The phraseology may be unfortunate, but at least it tries to make clear what all theologians who hold to an objective view believe needs to be made clear—that God is not faced with, nor does He deal with, an indefinite number of sinful men and women, regarded as so many separate atoms in respect of their sin and their guilt, but with a human race that has involved itself in sin. I cannot see that there is anything unreal in such a statement, any more than there is anything unreal (though there is a margin, small or large, of error) in speaking of " England " or " Germany," or any other unity which is not simply the sum of its component individuals. In this connexion one may refer to Dr. Rashdall's treatment of the relationship of retributive punishment to the objective view. It may be that all the supporters of that view believe that punishment is properly retributive; nevertheless, supposing that that belief were entirely abandoned, it does not follow that the Abelardian doctrine would be left in possession of the field; though the distinction between Anselm and the Reformers, the *aut satisfactio*

DR. RASHDALL ON THE ATONEMENT

aut poena is not to be pressed, yet a distinction there is. Mr. Grensted points out that Anselm deliberately refused the penal idea. The essence of the objective conception does not lie in the assertion of the necessity for penal suffering, but in the conviction that Christ in His Cross did something for us Godward, in the matter of sin, which we could not do for ourselves.

And finally, Dr. Rashdall does not at all do justice to the way in which the objective notion, including therein expiation and penal suffering, has been, not explained away, but spiritualized. One is surprised at times by the confidence with which the Dean brands that notion as immoral. The full rigour of his thought appears in the appendix on Dr. Dale, which, despite his tribute to Dr. Dale's Christian character, will cause both pain and regret. Now, even in Dr. Dale, there is nothing like a supposition of a need for so much penalty to match so much sin, nor is the substitutionary idea stated in a way that overlooks the all-important truth that redemption and reconciliation spring from love, not love from them. The whole theory of a transaction in which the Father and the Son were regarded as representing different interests, of a work which enables God to be gracious whereas before its accomplishment His attitude towards men was one simply of wrath and desire to punish, has passed almost clean away. At the same time there has developed a great insistence on that positive side of Christ's atoning work which is represented by the idea of the complete obedience of His will; in other words, the old distinction between the passive and active obedience has been merged in the thought that the death of Christ was not just something endured, but a work done, because all through that work the relationship of His will to the Father's cannot for a moment be overlooked. That does not do away with the expiatory and penal element; it does not mean that the thought of Christ as our substitute is wholly invalid; but it does away with mechanical reckonings, while leaving us able to say, in confidence that the words need offend neither our intelligence nor our conscience, that on the Cross Christ made "a full, perfect, and sufficient sacrifice, oblation, and satisfaction, for the sins of the whole world." It should in fairness be added that Dr. Rashdall does not, in his survey of Christian thought, go beyond the Reformation; nevertheless he does criticize both Dr. Dale and Dr. Denney, and one may ask whether he does not treat them both as though their doctrine were altogether more rigid and less spiritual than it is.

How acute the opposition is between Dr. Rashdall and the other writers whose works have been considered is obvious. Canon Hart and he are in agreement in their antipathy to Western theory, yet even at this point there is nothing like whole-hearted agreement, since Canon Hart objects to the emphasis laid upon the reparation made by Christ as man, whereas Dr. Rashdall sees in everything Christ did the work of a particular man, though a man completely united with the Logos. And if we leave Canon Hart out of account in points which are connected with the whole Western tradition, we shall see at every point fundamental differences, as to the moral nature of God and the demands resulting from it, as to sin and the

DR. RASHDALL ON THE ATONEMENT

character of its connexion with mankind, as to Christ and His relationship to man, as to biblical, or more precisely, apostolic inspiration and authority. Dr. Rashdall's soteriology takes its place as a close-knit view, a more radical and extensive Abelardianism, involving (less than Dr. Moberly's doctrine, but still involving) a whole theology. Were it widely accepted in the unflinching, uncompromising spirit in which it has been put forward, it would mean, despite the elements in some historic theories which could be used in its support, an enormous break with Christian tradition.

One other contribution to the subject must not be left unnoticed : Dr. Sanday's sermon on the Meaning of the Atonement, with which his last book, *Divine Overruling*,[1] closes. Those who remember how, in the great commentary on Romans, and in appreciation and criticism of Dr. Moberly and Dr. du Bose (though he conceded to du Bose important theological positions which he had formerly held), Dr. Sanday refused to give up that type of soteriology which has as its *locus classicus* in the New Testament Rom. iii. 24–26, will find the same spirit of desire to conserve, and not to reject, present in the sermon. Dr. Sanday sides with Dr. Denney and Dr. Moffatt in believing that the faith of the Early Church, in the atoning character of Christ's death, "had its roots in the consciousness that He was Himself called upon to play the part of the suffering servant of Jehovah described in the fifty-third chapter of Isaiah." At the same time, it

[1] *Divine Overruling*, by W. Sanday, D.D., F.B A (T. & T. Clark. 1920.) 6s. net.

would not be fair to claim Dr. Sanday's support for the dogmatic constructions of the objective idea which have been built up on the basis of the text of Scripture. That kind of dogmatic construction has clearly, in his opinion, been greatly overworked. And though he is prepared to defend the use of such words as " propitiation " or " expiation," the meaning which he attaches to them is at one with that given in the great systems only in so far as the same elementary conceptions are present in both. But whereas the creators of the systems, and St. Paul also, went beyond these elementary conceptions of a gift to gain the smile of God or acute sorrow for sin passing into act, Dr. Sanday stops there, not necessarily condemning further advance, but unwilling to make the road of dogmatic construction his own. And past constructions he does to this extent condemn, that " hints " in the Bible, which could be dogmatically developed, " were the wrong hints to make use of, and they were used in the wrong way." It will be realized that Dr. Sanday is concerned with method rather than with theory. Of Dr. Rashdall's insight into the Epistle to the Hebrews, and, by implication, into the Bible, as a whole, he speaks in terms of high praise; whether he would associate himself with Dr. Rashdall as a dogmatic theologian is another question to which there is not the material for an answer.

The statements and theories with which we have been engaged have the use, besides their own intrinsic interest, of throwing light upon the various points at which more than one road may be taken. There are, indeed, a large number of these in connexion with the doctrine of the death of Christ, far more than in connection with the doctrine of His Person. With regard to the latter doctrine, despite all the elaborate dogmatic constructions for which the last century was responsible, everything hinges on Phil. ii. 5-11, which I believe makes the issue clearer than any other New Testament passage, clearer than the prologue to the Fourth Gospel or than the great Christological section in Col. i. The Philippian passage is either (one cannot avoid the either . . . or in this judgment)—is either myth or concrete truth. The building up of a Christology independently of it is, in effect, to treat it as myth. But in soteriology there is no such immediate demarcation of types which may be related to one particular New Testament statement. Rom. iii. 24-26 does not provide the means for such a differentiation. Nor is there a straight line through from the New Testament to any later doctrine, Anselmic, Reformation, "moral influence," as there is from the evangelic portrait of Christ and the epistolary interpretation thereof to the doctrine of the Two Natures. To those who deny such a straight line in Christological theory, and point to the intrusion of other influences, it may at least be answered that the Greek and Latin Fathers were able to take the New Testament and depend upon it directly, with far less of their own theorizing imported, than was the case with the doctrine of the Atonement. All the interpretations of the Atonement had their appeal to Scripture, but it is impossible to overlook the amount of purely theoretical work involved in practically all of them, in, for instance, so crude a conception as that variant of the doctrine of the ransom to Satan, in which the devil, eager to seize the flesh of Christ, is caught in the mousetrap which represents the presence of Christ's divinity. Where the theoretical element is not present is in the Abelardian doctrine, but that is precisely because Abelard tried to make one scriptural idea—that of the love of God shed abroad in men's hearts (Rom. v. 5) —serve for soteriology, rather, as I have suggested, as the passage in Philippians serves for Christology ; but the difference is that whereas that latter passage does necessarily exhibit one doctrine, and, by direct implication, reject others, that on which Abelard relies does nothing of the sort : it goes no further than to claim that for it, in any true soteriology, a place must be found.

Now it is clear that a great unsettlement has come over both popular and theological thought in connexion with the Atonement, due to various causes, such as a realization of all that was morally indefensible in the statements of the historic theories, a new attitude towards the Bible as an authority for dogma, a changed interpretation of animal sacrifice, with a surrender of the idea of a rigid relationship of type and antitype in the Old and New Testaments. The position cannot be compared with that which obtained before the great constructions were made ; it is not possible to return to that time, for the history of the doctrine and all its effects block the way.

What seems to be necessary is a clearing of the ground. It may be possible to arrive at a real measure of unity with regard to the presuppositions underlying the attempt to construct a formal doctrine. Apart

DR. RASHDALL ON THE ATONEMENT

from this it is useless to expect anything more than a number of individual repetitions or experiments in the field of dogmatics. And there is grave danger at this point: granted the present theological atmosphere, and the present set of religious tendency, there will always be the risk of the most novel theories and the most brilliant exponents obtaining the fullest hearing, and running away with the sympathies of large sections of the Church. And when this happens the Church becomes too much of a debating society and too little of an accredited witness and trustee, which is already in considerable measure the case. A full agreement as to presuppositions is out of the question; on the lines of Dr. Rashdall's book hardly any common ground is to be found between Abelardianism as there expounded and interpreted, and any objective view. Dr. Rashdall writes as one convinced that here is a case of either . . . or.

But if Dr. Rashdall does not persuade us to make the clean sweep of objective soteriology which he has done, we are back in the undoubted difficulty of discovering a unity of formula which shall bear witness to a unity of doctrine, which, in its turn, shall testify to a common judgment and consequent progress at the various points at which possible roads divide. Now it is true enough that past history suggests the great difficulty of anything like a satisfactory unity of formula; and because that is the lesson of past history, unity of formula, in itself, is not something which appears to me to matter much; in Christology, where the history has been very different, unity of formula does matter. But it would be intolerable if we were forced to say that because we can have no unity of formula we can have no unity of doctrine, and because we can have no unity of doctrine we can have no unity of judgment upon and choice of the several roads which offer themselves. So what I would propose to do is to start from the other end, and try to see where unity of background or presuppositions is obtainable, and, to some extent, realized among all who hold to the objective theory. The establishment of such unity, as representing no temporal alliance among schools of theology in the face of what they all would regard as a common attack, but the conviction that the objective theory is grounded in principles of unchanging validity, would mean a great improvement on the present situation.

First, then, as to the moral character of the world-order. It is obvious that the work of Christ will have a close relationship to that character. According to the needs which seem to emerge when the world-order is morally valued, so will it be reasonable to see in that earthly climax of the self-revelation of God in Christ something which takes account of those needs, and leaves them no longer just what they were before. Among those needs is the desire for a revelation that in the struggle between good and evil God does not play the part of a neutral, but on the contrary guarantees the final triumph of good. If it is asked why this should not be left to the future, to a revelation to be made in a final Day of the Lord, the answer is that the moral character of the world-order and its final issue is something which concerns moral personalities

DR. RASHDALL ON THE ATONEMENT

now; for the question which is present with us is, In what sort of a world are we living? Doubtless this world includes many moral experiences of a tragic and evil kind; sin and guilt and their wages in suffering and punishment are actual facts. What is there to set against them? Repentance, moral betterment, the chastening and purgative results of suffering and punishment. But these experiences do not seem sufficient to give assurance of moral victory already present in the world-order, of an end in the future which cannot possibly fail to be attained: they do not confer security. That is, I will not say established in the only way, but best established on the basis of something in which complete moral victory is already present as an achievement which can never be reversed. The idea of a "finished work" is no valueless and immoral notion. A work in which the whole struggle between good and evil could be gathered up, and a settlement made which should create a new moral situation, would be inestimably valuable. That there is this morally creative power in the death of Christ regarded as objective atonement, which has its bearing, not only upon the individual in stimulating love and repentance, but upon the world-order in making it other than it was, sealing it as secured for a goodness which has come victoriously out of the strife with evil, is a judgment which at least tries to do justice to the facts. And as to every word which has been technically used to describe the work of Christ as atoning, "satisfaction," "reparation," "penal suffering," "expiation," we may approach them with the desire to know whether and how far they can find a place in a construction of the moral order of the world which is in no respect mere theory, but theory working in close relation to the moral experiences of mankind. And I think we may emphasize this—that the conception of the death of Christ as objective atonement, that is, as a finished work, is not a nonsensical conception which has its place only in an unreal universe, nor can any valid moral indictment be brought against it. Whatever may be said against certain ways of construing the objective work of Christ, the objection does not shatter the basis of the interpretation of the world-order, on which all those constructions depend. There are grounds on which the belief that in point of fact Christ's death was objective atonement, a " finished work," may be attacked, but I cannot see that it is properly arguable that if the belief is a true belief, it does not elevate our whole conception of the moral character of the world-order and God's action in respect of it.

Secondly, every doctrine of objective atonement implies a particular understanding of Christ's earthly ministry; that understanding will necessarily be affected by the belief in Christ as Messiah and Son of God. Now it does not appear extravagant to say that granted that belief, an interpretation of the death of Christ must be found which is not only intelligible in relation to the development of the historical situation in which it takes its place, but is also intelligible in relation to the counsels of God. In other words, we are bound, as St. Peter on the day of Pentecost was bound, to say more than that Jesus Christ was slain by the hands of wicked men : St. Peter spoke of His

DR. RASHDALL ON THE ATONEMENT 145

death as happening by the determinate counsel and foreknowledge of God: this agrees with the declaration of Christ Himself, that it was necessary for Himself to suffer many things and be crucified. To find a necessity, which has its roots in God's express will, for the death of One to Whom the name of Son of God uniquely belongs, may involve a difficult search, but it is a search entirely reasonable in itself. Even if, apart from the theology of St. Paul, the Early Church expressed itself with regard to the death of Christ in traditional formulæ which rested upon the use of a prophetical passage, and, apart from that, concentrated attention rather on the moral fruits of the Christian life, that by no means implies that the Church was unconscious of a divine necessity for Christ's passion. A coherent understanding of the earthly life and ministry of our Lord is, I allow, less easy when a sharp division is made, in the fashion of one tradition in the old dogmatic, between the active obedience of the ministry of work, with its doing of the will of God, and the passive obedience of the suffering upon the Cross. A passive consummation of an active ministry does present a difficulty. But just at this point the clearer vision which one associates with the writings of Dr. Forsyth helps us to correct this fault, by its perception of the real activity present in the Cross, the activity of a will set upon the confession of God's holiness in the midst of and throughout the endurance of suffering. This conception of Christ's active obedience does not, of course, involve a theory of objective atonement; it is compatible with theories of quite a different kind, but it can be held along with that objective view, and wards off the objection that when that view is held, Christ's work on earth is not regarded as, so to speak, all of one piece. I can understand the objection which is felt to such a standpoint as might be expressed in words like " Christ came into the world to die " ; but the force of the objection disappears if it is said " Christ came into the world to do the Father's will; that will involved His death." The death of Christ then takes its place as at once the climax of His active ministry, and, at the same time, as that new fact in which was adjusted the relationship between the holiness of God and the world's moral evil.

Then, thirdly, the death of Christ, conceived of as objective atonement, holds a unique place in connexion both with systematic theology and with Christian experience. And if one calls it not only unique but vital, that means no judgment upon individuals who take the matter quite differently. One is thinking of the Church as a whole, and of the possibilities of the future. What systematic theology needs is an adequate centre, and an adequate doctrine of final causes. It is concerned with God in respect of His action, and not simply of His being. And the action of God must be presented in an intelligible form, and as seeking particular ends. Now it is clear enough that what God seeks in relation to free personalities is a kingdom of good wills. We can hardly recall too often that most profound saying of Kant's that nothing within the world or outside it can be thought of as completely good, except a good will. But the idea of a kingdom of good wills does not shut out the idea of objective atonement, unless the action of God is conceived of as related merely to the future, operating through such inducements and helps as may seem to Him most serviceable for the moral end in view. In that case, such an action of God as is given in the doctrine of the Incarnation cannot be regarded as more than exemplary. But in that case, God's moral action on the world is limited by the extent to which the example which He has provided rouses men to the true moral life; and the defect of this result is that the moral centre of the world is not to be found in the action of God, but in the action of man. There is nothing equal to the grandeur of the old soteriology which held to a moral centre of the world called into existence by the action of God Himself working directly upon the whole moral situation, restoring its broken order as well as supplying new motives and powers for the future. To some extent it may be a valid complaint against the old systematic theologies that they inclined to emphasize the metaphysical rather than the ethical, a doctrine of substance rather than of action. But in so far as that was the case, it was not due to their objective soteriologies; these contained an implicit correction of such weaknesses, for an atonement which reveals in itself the moral action of God must throw light upon all other parts of the dogmatic scheme, if only it is treated with an understanding of its central position. And at a time when the notion of a struggling, suffering God, crude and unsatisfying as it is, shows how much is felt the need for a God Whose relation to the world shall be in some sense one of moral action, it would be a profound mistake to belittle a doctrine which sets the whole Christian revelation in the light of what God has done for the supreme moral purpose of a holy kingdom.

That the objective doctrine has been linked up with one great type of Christian experience would not be denied. One cannot say that either has been the creator of the other: certainly it is not right to say that experience has produced the doctrine by way of an immediate deliverance of the Christian conscience. But it is not unfair to say that if the objective doctrine were thoroughly discarded, the Church would be the poorer by the loss of some of the most strengthening and comforting experiences which ever come to Christian souls; and, more than that, an unique experience would disappear from the world. For the Church's appeal to the world is again and again made on the basis of the children's hymn, and it is not so easy to replace an appeal of that kind. If we had to stop singing

> There was no other good enough
> To pay the price of sin;
> He only could unlock the gate
> Of heaven and let us in,

we should be inevitably condemning as untrue (however defensible in the conditions of other days), not only the form but the substance of the Church's evangelizing and converting ministry. Christian experience is varied; one ought to beware of attempting to stretch the consciences and the feelings of all alike upon a Procrustean bed with which these must exactly correspond; but it is not improper to give weight to those experiences of forgiveness through the Blood of

Christ in which the Christian message, as a Gospel for sinful and guilty men, has come home so powerfully to unnumbered multitudes.

That the idea of atonement in any form which allows us to speak of a finished work introduces us to a region of profound mystery is certain. Yet it is none the less true that in the same idea is found an extraordinarily simple religious appeal. The elimination of the element of mystery would lead to no strengthening of that appeal. We have learnt to discard modes of expression that were intellectually and morally indefensible, and that is all to the good: we are legitimately suspicious of too great rigidity in theory, and of concentration upon any one formula. But we have no cause to be ashamed if we go on to say that neither intellect nor conscience compels us to cut ourselves off from the faith which saw an objective Godward value in the Cross of Christ, and that the heart which has its reasons bears witness that that is true.

VI

THE PERSON OF OUR LORD

It is the Christian contention that Christianity is the absolute religion. It is a contention with a double implication, that, on the one hand, there can be no true development of religion which will leave Christianity behind as a creed and life that has served many generations, but is, for all that, merely a stepping stone on the road to a more perfect religion in the future; on the other, that Christianity contains within itself all the potency for satisfying the religious needs of humanity in the fullness of their varied characteristics. It is not at all necessary to argue that the whole splendour of Christianity as the absolute religion has already been revealed; on the contrary, we can apply yet more widely and richly those fine and believing words which the old Pilgrim Father, John Robinson, spoke in reference to the Holy Scriptures: " The Lord hath yet more light and truth to break forth from His Holy Word "; but we are committed to the faith that the Word of God, which is the Gospel, will never be refined or sublimated into something that transcends our Christian understanding of it. Christianity is not one of

> the great world's altar-stairs
> That slope thro' darkness up to God.

It is the altar, the only true and perfect one. If a good example is required of what Dr. Liddon called the "Inspiration of Selection," though applied not to the contents of a biblical book, but to its place in the New Testament Canon, there is none better than the Epistle to the Hebrews. How great would have been our loss if the doubts which prevailed in the West as to that book had had their way and it had never taken its place alongside of the other New Testament Epistles! For in that letter the whole idea of the finality of Christianity is present and in control. It was intended to prevent some little community of perplexed Christians from slipping back to the preparatory, imperfect, typical level of Judaism. But the writer gives us something far more and grander than the answer to a particular emergency. What Stephen was trying to do when they broke in on his unfinished defence, and thought to answer the arguments by silencing the speaker, that the writer "to the Hebrews" accomplished. He presents with a dignity of style worthy of the grandeur of his subject the Christian philosophy of history. He works it out mainly in reference to the problem of true worship; his theme is that in God's revelation through the Son the reality of priesthood and sacrifice has been manifested. But obviously there can be no restriction of his thought to this sphere. Manifold as must be the extensions of his thought, the thought itself is simple and unmistakable: God has spoken once again and finally. I doubt if the writer would have been content with the well-intentioned but not very profound piety of the couplet which tells us how for other worlds God may have other words—

But for this world the word of God is Christ.

His philosophy of history is, after all, not simply a philosophy of this world's history and of this world's religion. Not less than St. Paul does he conceive of Christ's Lordship in the universe both before the Incarnation and after the Ascension.

Now, if Christianity is the absolute religion it must be so in virtue of its central and vitalizing principle. There must be the closest interaction between the finality of a religion, by which phrase we imply a comparison between its claims and the claims made by or on behalf of other systems in the same religious field, and its meaning. When we are busy with the meaning of a religion we are busy with its inmost core, with the centre which explains both its own growth as an organism and the outward extension of its power. Very illuminating in connexion with two of the great historic religions is the position at this point. At the heart of primitive Buddhism lay the message of freedom from all desire, and the attainment of that silence of Nirvana, where peace could at last be attained through the death of desire, of consciousness, and of personality. And though that early Buddhism has sustained profound changes in the course of its historical development in the East, the ideal of Nirvana—that is, of the extinction of consciousness—has still remained as the highest ideal attainable, though only a few can hope to attain to it. In other words, the highest form of the Buddhist doctrine of salvation is a salvation dominated by the principle of negation and elimination. And when one is in touch with a religious doctrine of salvation, one is in touch with its final promises and hopes; and then one is right at its

THE PERSON OF OUR LORD

centre. And the last note in this Buddhist doctrine is not of the transcendence of the limitations of humanity, but of the passing away of humanity.

Primitive Buddhism has everything to say about man, and, in effect, nothing about God. For the Buddha himself the relationship between God and man was not a problem which troubled him at all, and if his system is regarded as atheistic that is because whatever he thought about the existence of gods, he did not think that they were of any importance to man, or had anything to do with man's salvation. For Islam, on the other hand, the centre of religion resides in the sovereignty of Allah. It is a doctrine of sheer religious transcendence. But because of the rigorous and one-sided way in which this conviction dominates the whole Mohammedan creed, a vital relationship between God and man becomes impossible except in so far as, in the case of the Sufis, there has been a reaction in the direction of a mystical pantheism. Neither in the creed of Buddha nor in the creed of Mohammed, whether in the original form or in the religious development characteristic of them, can we recognize the presence of a vitalizing principle out of which could grow a religion beyond which it would not be necessary to look, a religion capable of answering to every call which might be made upon it, and possessed of a creative power grander and more mysterious than any life-force which a Bergson or a Bernard Shaw sees at work in the processes of natural evolution.

Now, if we turn to Christianity and ask what is its very core, what is that primal fact without which the religion loses both its meaning and its power, there can be no shadow of doubt as to the answer. It is given in a verse of the last chapter of the Epistle to the Hebrews, a verse which seems to stand almost curiously alone, but whose inclusion serves as some brilliant illumination, which lights up in a moment the whole of its environment and discloses the features of the country in so unmistakable a manner that the traveller treads with the certainty of knowledge, and has no longer to grope for a footing here or there, to try, and to turn back from, this or that alternative. " Jesus Christ," says the writer, " is the same yesterday and to-day, yea and for ever." If we could but unconventionalize our understanding of the New Testament, we should see in a moment, with the eyes of our mind truly enlightened, that into these tremendous words is packed the absoluteness of the only religion of which an absolute and final character can be asserted with any hope of a verification through experience. Let me put it like this : Jesus Christ came full of grace and truth, and that grace and truth were, and for ever are, final. He did not come from a dark background which holds in reserve further manifestations destined to overshadow even Him. If that were the case, it would be no more than a rhetorical turn, and illegitimate at that, to make His Person co-extensive with the whole past and the whole future. His arm would be shortened and He could not save— not everything and to the end. The ages to come would not be His ; He might have an interest in them, but only by so preparing for them that their crowns of glory might adorn the head of another, greater than Himself. He might be the Baptist's Christ and even

THE PERSON OF OUR LORD

ours, but not the King of the Ages, the Alpha and Omega, the unending Amen in Whom the music of all history and all life could reach its final and triumphant climax. And if anyone says that to leave the future open for some further manifestation, for what is called, though most inexactly, a further incarnation, need not affect the attitude of piety towards Jesus Christ to-day, I can but express my entire conviction that in such a case piety would find the very nerve of its devotion cut through, and would no longer be able to take upon its lips, either those words of Charles Wesley than which none in any native English hymn go deeper—

> Thou, O Christ, art all I want,
> More than all in Thee I find—

or those still profounder lines (if that is possible) of the *Dies Iræ*—lines in which St. Paul and St. Augustine would have beheld the reflection of the redemption-light that burned within their souls:

> Rex tremendæ maiestatis,
> Qui salvandos salvas gratis,
> Salva me, fons pietatis.

There are three conceptions to which adequate justice must be done in any religion which professes to be, or for which the claim is made that it is, the absolute religion: the conceptions of God, of man, and of the relationship between God and man. And of these three, the most difficult and critical is the conception of the relationship; for how to bring God and man together in such a way that neither is God lost in man, nor is man a mere instrument or, at best, slave in the presence of God—that is no easy problem to solve. But in primitive Christianity it was solved, we may say right away, in Jesus Christ. There was the new relationship, and the perfect one, in Him. Take some of the great problems which confront the worker in the fields of the philosophy of religion, problems of immanence and transcendence, of the Divine omnipotence, of the suffering of God. We are not nearly finished with the theory of these things yet, and the Church of New Testament times had not begun to concern itself with their theory. But that Church was certain that it possessed in Christ a full revelation, which provided the lines along which it would have asserted that these and similar problems, had they been debated at the time, found their solution. And the Christian contention was and is that it is the religion of true personal relationship between God and man, established and continuing through One in Whom the perfection of relationship between those two terms—" God," " man "—exists, because He is the perfection of both terms: He is perfect God and perfect man.

Here we are right at the centre of Christianity. The full content of that centre is indeed not yet apparent in what has so far been said. For the full content means the Person of Christ in all the greatness and mystery and glory of His experiences. Do let us remember that Christianity has nothing whatever to say about conceivable and formal relationships between God and man apart from Christ. The Church preaches Christ, and a philosophy only in dependence upon Him. It preaches One Whose Person

THE PERSON OF OUR LORD

is not an illustration of truths which exist independently of Him, but is creative of truth. That God and man are of one substance; that God is engaged in reconciling man to Himself; that the path of man on the road to consciously realized unity with God lies through the valley of the shadow of suffering and death, and climbs to the heights of victory, and vanishes at last into the heavens above, and conducts to a seat of honour in the heavenly places—all these may be propositions philosophically arguable and mystically appropriated, but they are not distinctively Christian, they do not reveal the Christian method, they do not explain and interpret the Gospel. In all the unceasing discussions about Christian origins, in all the attempted, and often valuable, separation of different strands in our primitive documents with a view to the elucidation of what lies behind them, there is at times a danger lest the unity of the New Testament as the reverberation in writing of a preached Gospel of salvation should weigh too lightly on our minds. People sometimes talk as though the issue concerning the Person of Christ were merely a problem of formal dogmatics in a particular sphere. No greater mistake could be made. The issue is dogmatically important, but religiously it is vital. No other foundation can any man lay save that which is laid —Jesus Christ. And the whole inner growth and development, and external extension, of Christianity as the religion which claims for itself finality is explicable, and of abiding absolute value, only because of that foundation. Take two indispensable activities of the Christian Church, its worship and its evangelizing or missionary zeal. They mean Christ, they proclaim Christ, they give Christ, Christ in the fullness of His Divine Sonship, in that fullness which includes all the humiliation of His bitter Passion, all the travail of His Cross, all the triumph of His Resurrection, all the royalty of His present reign. I come by accident upon a page in a book which I have just taken up, Dr. Forsyth's *The Person and Place of Jesus Christ*, and this is what I find written in his criticism of the view that all religion is evolution and no religion is final: " And so, with the end of any absolute or final religion, there is an end of much that troubles the world, for instance, of Missions at least. For Christian Missions cannot live upon improving the heathen, but only on passing them from death to life." And what is true here is true also of worship, and especially of the Eucharist. The potency of the Eucharist is not to be found in the fact that it is a banquet of religious fellowship, a pious commemoration, or even a mystical drama. It may be one or all of these, but that is not what matters. We could obtain all the benefits of such aspects of it in other ways—and many do. What matters in the Eucharist is the reality of the divine gifts—in other words, of the Gospel made available for men in a unique manner, so that Christ in the continual potency of His life, laid down in sacrificial death and taken again, becomes their Food. The mystery of the Eucharist is not, primarily, a mystery of dialectics and logic, but of life, of life imparted and life received, of spiritual realities spiritually discerned.

What I have been saying amounts to this, that the question of dogma with regard to our Lord's Person cannot be separated from, and is indeed derivative from, that centrality of His Person in the Christian religion which constitutes the Christian Gospel and is the foundation of the claim made for that religion that it is absolute religion. Dogma is to this extent secondary. But to say that is by no means to say that the dogmatic issue is of comparatively slight importance. On the contrary, it is closely linked up with the religious. The religious issue affects directly worship and work; the dogmatic affects them through the reaction upon them of thought. You cannot split man up into departments; you cannot revive at this point the old psychology of human nature as constituted in so many faculties; you cannot disconnect the intelligence from the emotions and the will. The impossibility, in its reference to the Person of Christ, has been put quite simply and, I would maintain, quite incontrovertibly, by an eminent Scottish theologian, Dr. H. R. Mackintosh: " One who is simply human to the mind cannot remain adorable to the conscience and the heart." The Christian response to Christ, the response of the individual believer and of the Church, is congruous with the Nicene Creed. The two fit one another. And that fitness emerges all along the line, not artificially, but by way of natural correspondence, in historic Christianity. It is an intellectual correspondence, and not simply an æsthetic one. The pre-existent Christ, the Christ born of a Virgin, the Christ of the unparalleled teaching and of the mighty works, the Christ Who made the Cross an altar, Who first hallowed the grave, and then left it empty, is the Christ Who explains Christianity. It is that Christ Who is the creative and redeeming Christ in the Church's life and discipleship.

I am not saying that those who do not share, at least in its fullness, the mind of the Church as to our Lord's Person have made no contribution towards the living apprehension of Him. There are scholars who would fall within this class from whose work much is to be learned, not only because they are scholars, but because of what they know of the grace and truth which have been manifested and are alive in Christ. But always one must remember that we are concerned with an issue which goes far beyond the fields of scholarship or of personal piety. It is an issue which must work itself out in consequences far-reaching and subtle for the future both of the Church and of the world. And the relationship of Christ to the Church and to the world can never be determined as though He were the greatest and most splendid and holiest of private persons, without a fundamental change in the Gospel.

But it is sometimes said or implied that there is no cause at the present time for any special anxiety, that to make the past more intelligible to the present through restatement or a fresh setting is not to abandon the past, and that the Nicene Creed is one thing and any particular interpretation of it another, and that (to take up one contention which has been made and defended) to believe in the Deity of our Lord and that He is the second Person in the Holy Trinity does not necessarily imply that His existence from all eternity as the Divine Word or Son was an existence carrying with it a consciousness distinct from the consciousness of God the Father. In fact, it has been quite clearly and strongly maintained that if, when we think of God, we think of more than one centre of consciousness, we do, however unintentionally, give up the belief in the unity of God. I do not propose on this occasion to enter on the technicalities, theological and philosophical, of the subject. I would not deny that those who affirm the truths of the Incarnation and of the Deity of our Lord, while they reject the idea of the pre-existence of the Son of God as a distinct personality, do so with the conviction that they are doing justice to those great words and to the historic Christian Gospel. Nor is the warning against believing in more than one God to be disregarded. But I find it impossible to doubt that the effect to-day of a doctrine of Christ's Person which abandoned the conception of distinct personal pre-existence, and sought, apart from that conception, to explain the incarnation of the Divine Word or Son in Jesus, would be, both in the case of members of the Church who made no profession of exact theological knowledge and interest, and in the case of those who could be described as theologians or theological students, most seriously prejudicial to the faith that our Lord is perfect God as well as perfect man. For that faith, and the formulas of the Church, both of Nicæa and of Chalcedon, mean that our Lord was God and became man. This is the meaning of the historic Catholic Christology, as Dr. Headlam has emphasized in some pages of great importance written five years ago.[1] And he is interested in pointing out that the Catholic Christology, even when expounded technically and in detail, represents

[1] In his preface to Dr. Relton's book, *A Study in Christology*

the constant belief of the ordinary religious man, who " believes simply that God came down upon earth and lived as man ; that He was really God and really man." Now I do not believe that the type of Modernist Christology which I have had in mind expresses the meaning either of the historic faith or of the ordinary religious Christian man or woman to-day. Nor do I believe that it has the essential quality of staying-power, any more than the attempt which was once made to say that Christ had the value of God, and to leave the matter there. But the matter would not be left there. People will insist on going on to ask, " When you say that Christ has the value of God, do you mean that He really is God ? " And if the implicit meaning, the logic of the position, has all the time been that Christ is not God, that implicit meaning will some day become explicit and undeniable. After all, there is a limit to the possible explanations of such words as " Incarnation " and " Deity," and our present troubles and difficulties are not concerned simply with different explanations of the same agreed beliefs. It is easy to look at the matter in this way, but it is not the true way. We are concerned with the beliefs themselves, whether they are believed, and not merely how they are understood. And it is not an unreal danger that the words may be retained, while the faith which they are intended to conserve is strained out of them. It is a danger which is likely to beset to an increasing degree a Protestantism which does not feel at home with the Nicene Creed and sits loose to the sacramental system.

There is a word which expresses the positive, objective side of Christianity, that side on which Christianity

THE PERSON OF OUR LORD 163

appears as the Gospel of Salvation, more adequately than any other. It is the word " Grace," a word with deep roots in the Bible and a long history in Christian thought, a word susceptible of misuse and of unintelligent use, but a great word, a word of achievement and a word of promise. When it is truly used it lifts Christianity clean off the level of philosophical speculation and of natural religion, and Christianity is manifested as revelation from God and redemption by God. For Grace is the love of God in active exercise on behalf of sinful men. You lose the width of the scope of Grace and the profundity of its penetration unless you bring in that adjective " sinful." The Gospel is a Gospel for a perishing world and for men who have no true life except they have the true God. For the river of life proceeds from out of the throne of God, and as it flows it heals and blesses, and there is no wilderness so desolate and dreary which may not be changed by its waters into a garden of the Lord. So is Christ, our Lord, in the world and with men. So He works through the Church, which is His body. And the Church, in loyalty to that precious Blood of His Cross whereby He purchased her for ever, the Church which has no standing, no rights, no powers save those which are all of His Grace, knows Who He is and answers, " My Lord and my God."

VII

THE GOSPEL AND THE PERSON OF OUR LORD

IN the opening chapter of his book entitled *An Introduction to the Study of Comparative Religion*, Dr. F. B. Jevons has something to say on the subject of resemblances and differences between religions which seems to me opportune and important. He points out that while the readiness to compare Christianity with other religions, and to find points of similarity and even of identity is a commendable feature of our times, and is a sign not of weaker but of a stronger faith in Christianity, yet there is a danger in the discovery of likenesses of overlooking differences, a danger of emphasizing unity in religions to such an extent that the highest form of religion may come to be regarded as possessing no other content than what is already present in the lowest. This danger, which Dr. Jevons, as an expert in the science of religion, points out as liable to lead to false conclusions in one of the departments of that science, is not absent from other fields of theological study. The resemblances between the moral and religious teaching of Jesus and previous or contemporary Jewish or Greek ethic have been pressed so far that the paradoxical conclusion has seemed imminent that, after all, Jesus was not really a very remarkable Teacher. Paradoxical it is to imply that those (not all orthodox Christians) who have bowed before Him as the Supreme

GOSPEL AND PERSON OF OUR LORD 165

Teacher have, all unawares, been looking at Him through magnifying glasses. On a good deal of easy-going talk of this kind Wellhausen's dry epigram is the best criticism (though I have not his exact words) : —" Everything that Jesus said is in the Talmud—and how much besides."

Again, the relationship between St. Paul's doctrine of redemption, sacramentalism, and piety, and the utterances of the mystery-religions is being worked for all it is worth—and a good deal more. It would be an extraordinary thing if, amid the luxuriant, but by no means always valuable, fertility of the religious experiences, practices, and conceptions of the world about the time when St. Paul lived, no striking parallels with what we read in the Apostles' letters could be adduced. There are resemblances in words, and, on occasions, in the thought lying behind the words. But the religion of St. Paul is of a very different kind from the religion offered in the contemporary cults of Isis and Attis ; the leading impulses are different, the dominant ideas are different, and the differences both in these formative forces and in the developed results are not explicable as variations on one religious theme, or sub-species emerging from one specific type of religion. And here again one must bear in mind how much in true religion depends on the power to omit and to exclude. St. Paul and the primitive Church possessed that power to a remarkable degree. It was a sign of great tact and judgment . and in this is to be seen one of the greatest contrasts between the religion of the Church and the religions and cults of contemporary paganism.

Now the tendency to look for similarities rather than differences is natural enough. Every scholar in every subject must desire to bridge gaps, to discover connexions, to reduce the number of phenomena which challenge and perplex by their apparent isolation. And the Church which in the second century resolutely held on to the Old Testament and refused, despite difficulties and attacks which pressed both from the Jewish and from the Greek and Oriental side, to cut itself off from its Hebraic roots, is no more committed to such an interpretation of Christianity as a new religion as would deny that the past to which it succeeded prepared for it and the present in which it grew contributed to it, than it is committed to the affirmation of any permanently baffling break between the inorganic and the organic. Nevertheless, the new may not be as adequately understood and valued when it is looked at as continuous with the old as when it is set in contrast with the old. In any great movement the victorious thing which has the promise of the future that it may mould it according to its mind is the life-force which is *its* life-force, the immanent spirit which bears witness against the attempt to interpret the world and life exclusively along the lines of mechanism and to deny all freedom.

We shall beware, then, of overdoing the thought, the truth, of the resemblance between Christianity and other religions, theologies, and moral systems with which comparisons may be possible. It is no use gaining for Christianity whole series of even worldwide connexions, if, in the process, we lose its soul. And the soul of Christianity resides in its Gospel.

Christianity is the Gospel; when we speak of the Gospel we mean, or should mean, not an element in Christianity, not its religious appeal, not a scheme of salvation, but Christianity in its essential and total character. There is not something—the Christian religion—in which the Gospel is to be found here and there. The Gospel permeates and penetrates everywhere, in Christian doctrine, morals, institutions, worship. If you forget this you are in constant danger of regarding Christianity as *a* religion instead of as *the* religion, religion at its final stage, absolute religion. Christianity as theology, law, culture, ethic can be grouped and pigeon-holed with the dexterity and precision which are often such valuable instruments in the science of religion as well as in the natural sciences. And if the distinctive character of Christianity as Gospel is hidden away there will be little to prevent the science of religion being conceived of as just a branch of natural science. Nothing, indeed, can stop this attempt, and the danger that lies so near that many people, believing that religion has been explained, will conclude that it has thereby been exploded; but we shall be in a much better position to deal with the whole situation if we have maintained a firm and intelligent hold of the Gospel character of Christianity.

What should we mean by this word " Gospel " on which so much stress is to be laid? Let us look at the way in which the word is used in the New Testament. It is a word of the Epistles rather than of the Gospels, and its first appearance, if we adopt the most usual chronological order of the Epistles, is in 1 Thess. i. 5—" Our Gospel came to you not with mere words, but also with power and with the Holy Spirit, with ample conviction on our part " (Moffatt). This passage by itself does not give us the clue to the point of attachment and content of the εὐαγγέλιον, the good news which St. Paul and his companions had proclaimed at Thessalonica, but the case is very different elsewhere. In this same letter, in iii. 2, the Gospel is spoken of as the Gospel of Christ, where " of Christ " refers to the purport of the Gospel ; it is not simply good news about Christ, but good news whose whole content is Christ, good news which is Christ. This phrase " the Gospel of Christ " reappears in each one of the second group of Epistles, and also in the Philippian letter. The fullest and most impressive passage is, however, one from which those exact words are absent, while the significance attaching to them is richly given. I refer to the majestic opening of the Epistle to the Romans. There the Apostle speaks of himself as " set apart for the Gospel of God (which he promised of old by His prophets in the holy scriptures) concerning His Son." He means by the Gospel of God not the Gospel which has God as its subject, but the Gospel which takes its origin from God ; and this Gospel, whose coming God had vouched for through the mouth of the inspired prophets of the Old Testament, had been fulfilled in Him Who was both Son of David and Son of God, in Jesus Christ our Lord. For St. Paul the good news means that God has brought His promises to pass ; the culminating hope of the sacred scriptures is no longer a hope. The Messiah has come. But it would be a mistake to suppose that for St. Paul the Gospel is a Gospel simply by way of fulfilment; there is for him far more of newness, far more of paradox in the Gospel than is allowed for in such an idea. It is only necessary to read the third chapter and the first few verses of the fourth chapter of the Second Epistle to the Corinthians in order to correct any false ideas at this point. The glory of the new covenant of which he is the minister is not a mere prolongation of the glory of the old. The old glory faded with the coming of Christ: there is a glory about the revelation of Jesus as the Messiah which is veiled from those who have no eyes except for the old. It is the actual lasting glory of Christ which St. Paul preaches, the glory of His Person, and of His Person especially as revealed in the deep shadows of the Cross and the triumph of the Resurrection. St. Paul's Gospel is always the Gospel of action and achievement, a Gospel in which what man may hope from God and God may do for man is not viewed as destined to reach its climax in the far-off end of a process that gradually works itself out in the tangled skein of human life and history, but as already given in all that tremendous condensation of the Divine purpose, as of a river that suddenly narrows and deepens its waters in a rocky gorge, in the fact of Christ.

Now I know what is sometimes said—this is Paul and not Jesus, and Paul misinterpreting, giving us not the Gospel of the Kingdom of God which Jesus preached, but a Gospel of Jesus instead. Well, there is no doubt that the Apostle burnt all his boats when he wrote Gal. i. 6–9: if he was fundamentally wrong in his Gospel, we can hardly save him from his own repeated anathema by maintaining that he was right as against the Judaizers. What then are we to say about the Gospel in the Gospels ? I think that three points appear for consideration.

Firstly, the evidence from the use of the word " Gospel " is of an almost surprising character. Take St. Mark, our earliest Gospel: the non-Marcan appendix to the Gospel being omitted, our Lord uses the expression three times, in i. 15, xiii. 10, and xiv. 9. In not one of these passages is the Gospel defined ; it is spoken of absolutely—" believe in the Gospel," " the Gospel must be preached," " wherever the Gospel is preached." In the first chapter the Gospel is brought into close relationship with the approach of the Kingdom of God, and it is most natural to find in this fact the purport of the good news ; but in the two latter cases, whatever " the Gospel " may mean it certainly cannot mean the immediate advent of the Kingdom. In St. Matthew's Gospel, the words " believe in the Gospel " are absent from the passage which corresponds to the Marcan verse which tells of the beginning of the preaching of Jesus : on the other hand, in the apocalyptic discourse in St. Matthew xxiv, parallel to St. Mark xiii, " the Gospel," which is St. Mark's phrase, becomes " this Gospel of the Kingdom " : when it has been preached all over the world the end will come. In the account of the anointing at Bethany St. Matthew closely follows St. Mark, only changing " the Gospel " into " this Gospel." There can be no doubt that St. Matthew is more inclined to connect the Gospel closely with the Kingdom than is St. Mark. While St. Mark opens his writing with the words " The beginning of the Gospel of Jesus Christ," and speaks of Jesus as coming into Galilee " preaching the Gospel of God," St. Matthew says He went through Galilee, " preaching the Gospel of the Kingdom," and repeats the expression in ix. 35. St. Luke never uses the substantive in his first treatise, but the verb " to preach the Gospel" occurs several times, and, both as used by our Lord and by the Evangelist, in iv. 43 and viii. 1, has as its object the words " the Kingdom of God." But in vii. 22, in the reply to the Baptist's question as to whether Jesus is the expected Messiah, St. Luke's report of our Lord's words, in which the Baptist may find the true answer, undoubtedly includes (there is some uncertainty about the text in the Matthaean parallel), in quotation from Is. lxi. 1, " the poor have the Gospel preached to them." The meaning may be, as Dr. Plummer interprets, that the invitation to enter the Kingdom is extended to the poor, but it should be noted that the Gospel is not simply connected with the Kingdom as good news of the coming of the Kingdom, but with the Messianic age and the presence of the Messiah. If Jesus was no more than a herald, proclaiming good news of the approaching Kingdom, then He was no more in His own Person part of the good news than an ambassador is personally relevant to the message which he brings. But the evidence which we possess in our Gospels as to the meaning of the Gospel, where the word is used, is neither abundant enough nor clear enough to compel such a conclusion.

Then, secondly, if the Person of Jesus is, so far as His own teaching and character during His public ministry and His training of the disciples are concerned, no part of the Gospel which He preaches, the Gospels are very extraordinary documents. For it is at least hard to maintain that Jesus, Who is so much the central Figure in the Gospels that everything exists, everyone exists, in relation to Him, is central only as herald or ambassador might be central while delivering a message entrusted to him. Nor is it adequate to say that He is central as a plenipotentiary, who would be more truly central than an ambassador. The plenipotentiary, after all, is but for a time, and Jesus never represented Himself as but for a time. As Messiah, Son, Sacrifice, Judge, King, His significance transcends time. The literary analysis of the Gospels does not enable us to make a sharp disjunction between the Gospel and the Person of Jesus. It is in the common source of the sayings of Jesus, which we can trace through a comparison of those sayings in St. Matthew and St. Luke, that we find how great a thing it is to know the Son, so great a thing that the Father alone possesses it ; how great a thing it is to know the Father, so that only the Son Who possesses it is able to impart it to others. Can this Son form no part of the Gospel which He preaches? Is the Son of Man Who forgives sins, Who overrides the law of the Sabbath, Who gives His life a ransom for many, Who shall come to judge in glory, and sit upon His throne, so much less than the message which He brings that really He is quite outside it ? Of course it is tremendous—far more so than we often realize—

GOSPEL AND PERSON OF OUR LORD

that Jesus should have spoken in this way, and I think I can understand how scholars like Bossuet are drawn to reject such sayings as reflecting the mind of the later Church read back into the words of Jesus. But to understand is not to justify. There are times when some even of our great critics deal with the documents in which the words of Jesus are contained as though they were endowed with some superior and esoteric principle of knowledge, enabling them to affirm with the utmost confidence what, in those sources, can, and what cannot be true.

Thirdly, to the Gospel in the Gospels belong the climax of the Gospels. We ought to realize more than we always do the importance of the Resurrection as a principle of interpretation. That the Resurrection throws a bright light upon the Cross is obvious ; the value of the Cross as an atoning sacrifice is not created by the Resurrection, but it is through the Resurrection that we gain the power to understand the Cross. But the Resurrection illuminates the whole life of Jesus and not the Cross alone. It is impossible to separate the significance of the Resurrection from the significance of Him Who rose again. That no separation was made by the Apostolic Church at its very beginning is made clear by the narrative and speeches of the early chapters of Acts. There we find the way opened to a true emphasis—on the truth of the Resurrection, and that it was the Resurrection of Jesus. That the heart of the Gospel of Jesus is to be found in what He taught rather then in those awful and triumphant experiences—the experience of the Cross, the experience of the Resurrection, which are the focal points of the greatness and the mystery of His Person—is logically justifiable only on the basis of a consciously or unconsciously humanitarian Christology, which cannot allow of any real unveiling of the supernatural in Christ, is ill at ease with any doctrine of the Cross which goes beyond a deeply moving manward appeal, and is ready to interpret the Resurrection as the manifestation to the disciples, whether through vision or through inward assurance, of the survival of the spirit of Jesus. The Gospels themselves do not give us, if we take them as a whole and lay the weight of our understanding where the weight of their interest is to be found, a Gospel from which we can omit the Person, the Cross, and the Resurrection of Jesus Christ our Lord. They do not overthrow St. Paul's Gospel—they explain it.

This Gospel whose subject is the Lord's Person in all the fullness of the Lord's work (which means that the Church cannot be overlooked when we are thinking of what the Gospel includes) is the life of all religion, of all theology which in any true sense deserves the name of Christian. It is that Gospel which Christian faith affirms when it is bold to say with St. Paul that God was in Christ reconciling the world to Himself. On it is based the profoundly important fact in Christian theology, which is also Christianity's greatest contribution to the philosophy of religion, the more intimate personalizing of all the relationships between God and man. For the Person of Christ is all that God can be to man, all that man should be to God. Nor can there be any Gospel which possesses the character of real good news save one that emphasizes the

GOSPEL AND PERSON OF OUR LORD 175

reality, the value, and the permanence of personality both in God and in man ; nor can we rightly speak of redemption unless it be redemption not from, but of and to personality. A Christian Logos-theology which practises a detachment from the historic Person of Jesus is a less than Christian theology. It is no answer to this to say that the bearing of the Gospel at this point was not appreciated in the Church during the centuries when the orthodox doctrine of the Person of Christ was being fixed. For, in the first place, it is quite clear that in so far as this is true the Church suffered thereby ; secondly, while the philosophical idea of personality was still in its infancy the rich importance of the conception of the redemptive self-revelation of God in a historic, personal life could not be fully realized ; and, thirdly, the Church, with whatever of inadequacy, was still moving, thinking, and defining on the right lines. It is still on those lines that we are called upon to interpret the Gospel, to carry them further, and to enjoy a fuller light while doing so, but not to reverse them.

The Gospel of the Person and Work of Christ at times appears to us as a problem. But it also becomes for us the solution of all problems. And it does so by bringing us into a new world in which we have our part as a new creation, blessed with a new life. How full of the prophet's power to reveal truth are Browning's words :

> That one face, far from vanish, rather grows,
> Or decomposes but to recompose,
> Become my universe that feels and knows.

There is a sentence in one of the published letters

of the late Dr. James Denney, that great Scottish theologian, who was so much at home in the New Testament, especially where it is deepest and most life-giving, which seems to me to make the religious and Christian issue, with which we are all concerned, perfectly plain. " I don't believe," he writes, " that the Christian religion—let alone the Church—can live unless we can be sure of (1) a real being of God in Christ ; (2) the atoning death ; (3) the exaltation of Christ."

This is the Christ of Whom the Church is sure : and having that Christ the Church has, we have, all things. He is God's best gift to us, the gift in which the Giver gives Himself. And to have that best gift is to have the Gospel.

VIII

THE HOLY SPIRIT IN THE CHURCH

In the Apostles' Creed we say " I believe in the Holy Ghost," and immediately follow on with " the holy Catholic Church." This close association of the Church with the Spirit is very significant. We come to the end of the statement of our faith in the Divine Persons, the Father, the Son, and the Holy Ghost, and continue, not with the recitation of any particular blessings which God bestows upon the Christian soul, but by proclaiming the existence, the sacredness, and the greatness of the social and corporate side of Christianity. We speak of it, not as an ideal towards which we press, but as a reality here with us in the world. We speak of it, and of the Communion of Saints, which has so much to do with it, as the society in which the blessings are to be found which become the blessings of each individual Christian, one by one. Forgiveness, resurrection, eternal life—these are blessings which each Christian soul may enjoy, not indeed apart from other souls, and yet in a quite real and necessary sense, each for itself and as itself. My soul is my soul, and never, to all eternity, will it be your soul. But before the Creed says anything which brings in the thought of individual blessings, it speaks of that society of Christian souls, that home within which the Christian blessings are most surely to be found: it speaks of the Holy Catholic Church.

Now you may well say that I have been reading a good deal into this short article of the Creed. And yet all that I have been doing is to try to see what it means that the article of belief in the Church comes just where it does. The fact that before we pass from our faith in the Father, the Son, and the Holy Ghost to our faith in blessings which are gifts from God to man, we stop to say that we believe in something which does not fall exactly into either group, is a remarkable fact, and we must try to understand and interpret it. For this position which the Creed assigns to the Church is one which to large numbers of Christians would not be at all a matter of course. That after we have given our witness to the richness of our belief in God by associating faith in the Holy Ghost with faith in the Father and the Son, we should immediately pass to the thought of the Church—there are many good Christians who, if they compare the Creed with their own private ideas, must find this very strange.

And yet so far is this emphasis upon the social and corporate aspect of religion from being something quite peculiar to Christianity or to one particular type of Christianity, that it is found very early indeed in the history of religion. For in primitive religion the god of this or that tribe is likely to deal, whether in anger or in graciousness, not with individual members of the tribe, but with the tribe as a whole. The morality, such as it is, however thin its substance, is the morality of the tribe; an individual who acts

THE HOLY SPIRIT IN THE CHURCH 179

against it may bring down the wrath of the god on the whole tribe, which is, as it were, responsible to the tribal god for the preservation of the tribal customs. And the extent to which this thought of the importance of a society obtained in Jewish religion is made plain enough in the Old Testament. Indeed, the outstanding problem of Old Testament religion was how to secure for the individual a due sense of his own religious value, responsibility, and destiny in view of the immense strength of the corporate idea.

The position, then, of the Church in the Creed is not one for which in older religion there has been no preparation. But can we find a special reason for the mention of the Church immediately after the mention of the Holy Ghost ? Can we say that there is something specially fitting in the closeness to one another of these two articles of the Creed ?

Well, think of that great chapter in which, for the first time in his letters, St. Paul admits us to his vision of the Catholic Church (1 Cor. xii.). In that chapter there is a grand double thought. The former part of the thought is that the Spirit is one, and at the same time manifests Himself in the different spiritual gifts— wisdom, powers of healing, prophecy, and so on—with which different Christians are endowed. The latter part of the thought is that the differences in faculties, powers, and functions which exist among Christians do not prevent Christians from being one body. The unity of the Holy Spirit faces outwards and becomes the source of all these manifold excellencies among Christians ; but these excellencies are not the property of any individual, they belong to the one body, and face inwards to it. To the body each new Christian is joined ; to its excellencies he adds whatever is the Spirit's gift to him. But, at the very outset of the Christian life, it is by the Spirit that he has been baptized into the body—a vitally important idea, as it is a fact, since it involves the closest connexion between the Spirit and the body, so that the great gift of the Spirit, which stands at the beginning of the religious life, is the gift of unity with the body. If, later on, in writing to the Ephesians, St. Paul was to put in the forefront of the great Christian unities the one body and the one Spirit, that is all prepared for in the Corinthians' chapter. One cannot be wrong in saying that for him the reality of the one body which is the Church corresponds in a quite natural way, though (if I may be allowed the expression) it is the naturalness of the supernatural, to the reality of the one Spirit.

Thus the unity of the Church, so far from being an accidental attribute of the Church, is one of the great marks or notes of the Church whereby the Church is to show that she is the body which the Spirit fills with His power, and to which He gives the helps and the graces of the many members. And I cannot allow that there is any perversion of unity into uniformity if one says that, granted the idea of the unity of the Church, unity ought also to be present in such characteristic expressions of the Church's life as the Creed, the ministry, and the sacraments.

It is a magnificent vision to which we are admitted when we open our eyes to the vast richness and significance of our belief in the Church. For it is by this

THE HOLY SPIRIT IN THE CHURCH

belief that we realize that Christian doctrine does not make its appeal to the intellect or even to the heart of Christians who stand aloof from one another, until they join together in a society of their own making ; but we learn Christian doctrine in the Church. Here we learn to believe in the Father and the Son and the Holy Ghost, in creation and redemption and sanctification, and in that new creation itself, the first fruits and final glory of the precious Blood shed on Calvary, the garden in which the soul is watered with the dew and warmed with the sunshine of God's heavenly grace, the home which is ever being enriched and beautified by the trophies which its children bring into it, above all by the memorials of themselves which they leave behind to the home, of the lives lived within it and inspired by its teaching, lives of enduring faith, of heroic adventure, of deepening holiness. Such is the Church, not that it is or can be here and now the whole fullness of the vision. For the Church grows into what it is God's purpose that the Church should become. You cannot understand or value the Church aright unless you take together these two facts—the Church is given, and the Church grows ; it is God's free, gracious, Spirit-filled gift to us, and our penitent, striving, all-grateful response to God. It is not easy, you will say, to hold these two aspects together. No, but you must have both, that you may have all the inspiration which comes from the knowledge that you are of the Church, sharing in the wealth of the Church's life, drinking of the living waters which tell of the presence of the Spirit in the Church; and all the responsibility which is the child of the remembrance that the Church does really depend, in however small a degree, on your endeavours, your sacrifices, your capacities for suffering, your fresh springs of joy.

One of two evils may easily beset the life of the Christian : formalism, convention, mechanical routine on the one hand ; vagueness, disorder, waste on the other. Here you see a hard efficiency, limited in outlook and range, scarcely conscious of the great mountain peaks and the distant horizons—the type of mind for which the problem for religion is no more than the problem of a jig-saw puzzle : the pieces are all to hand, and the only business is that of fitting them into one another. And there you have an enthusiasm which bubbles up from the shallows of a mind and experience which know little of the great deeps of sin, and of God's atoning goodness which has gone deeper still, which judges in terms of individual preferences and impulses, picks and chooses among ideas and purposes as though religion meant a lot of beliefs and practices, jumbled together incoherently like articles in a bran-pie at a bazaar, and each person must take what he finds most helpful, and feel no further responsibility than that. Of course, you will never find either type quite at its worst, but the existence of those two types at all shows the harm which results when belief in the Holy Spirit and belief in the Holy Church do not walk hand in hand. It is not simply a question of having the one and not the other ; but the overlooking, neglect, practical abandonment of either belief reacts gravely upon the other. The Spirit and the Church possess a real and divine union. It is the Spirit and the Bride together which bid the

THE HOLY SPIRIT IN THE CHURCH

Christian soul to come to the waters of life ; and that real union, a union in which we see the hand of God Himself, is a union which must be real for us too.

There are three lines along which we may look in order to see the meaning of the dwelling of the Holy Spirit in the Church. First, the line of the Church's doctrine and theology. I think partly of those great dogmatic utterances which we have in the Creeds, partly of Christian theology as a continually living and growing science. I am sure that amid the anxious restlessness of so much of modern religious thought we ought to find a true rest for our minds in the assurance that the Holy Spirit does lead the Church forward into all truth. There are wonderful powers of growth and of recovery. There is an instinct for true proportion and balance. So long as the unity of the Church remains broken, the doctrinal tasks of the Church can be handled only sectionally, but we are indeed slow of imagination if the magnificence of the Christian view of God and the world, as something which really exists, and exists as a great temple of truth and not as a battered ruin, does not deeply move us. There is a Catholic Creed, a Creed which lives on, thank God, where the Catholic view of the ministry and Catholic sacramental practice, which seem to us to go so naturally with the Creed, are of rather small account. I do not say that there are not questions of real difficulty with regard to Christian doctrine, with regard, for instance, to the view we ought to take of doctrinal decisions and doctrinal formularies which have not been the result of a deliberate concentration of the mind of the whole Church upon some debated question, and I would venture to say that it is not necessarily a proof of being a good Catholic to desire to extend the area of exact dogmatic decisions. But when I remember that there is a Christian view of God and the world; when I remember how that view, though in a true sense given in the New Testament, has yet been won for our use through controversies of a very difficult and very exacting character, controversies of which it must sometimes seem as though nothing good could come; when, looking back from the higher ground to which the future has brought us, I can see how, again and again, in the disputes which to some seem so useless and barren concerning the Person and the Natures of our Lord, any other decision than that to which the Church came would have worked itself out into utterly disastrous consequences for the Christian Religion—then what can I do but affirm, and with profound joy, that the Church has in truth been guided by the Holy Ghost, and that the one doctrine concerning the mystery of life which seems to me to have the power to satisfy our minds and hearts represents no merely human achievement, but that through the voice of the Church can be heard the speech of the Holy Ghost?

Then, secondly, along the line of what the Church teaches concerning right and wrong, and of all its wealth of holy lives, we pass to the conviction that it is only the presence of the Holy Spirit in the Church which explains the special quality of Christian goodness. We may feel this, especially when we read of or converse with someone who has obviously penetrated far within the secret chambers of true saintliness.

To me there comes a sense of the immense evidential value of the Christian life, both as an achievement which, in the heroes and saints of the Church, rises up and refuses to be denied, and as the ideal which challenges us all. That the saints really mean nothing at all, so far as the truth about life goes, is for me not only an utterly intolerable, but an utterly ridiculous thought. That as the saints have understood life and lived it, so essentially life is, that conclusion and that alone satisfies my reason. Wherever the flame of Christian holiness soars heavenwards and illuminates all around it with its pure and ardent light, there is the sign of the fire that has fallen from heaven, the fire of the Holy Ghost. Wherever there is true goodness, there is the Spirit of God; but in certain kinds and manifestations of goodness His presence is, as it were, more visibly displayed. As in the case of the Church's doctrine, I do not mean that there are no perplexities. The holiness of the Church has been a flower which evil weeds within the Church have too often tried to strangle. And the zeal for holiness itself has not always been a zeal according to knowledge. But the more one sadly admits all this, the less it is possible to reduce to a naturalistic level the amazing reality of the holiness which has sprung up and thrived—and does so still—within the Church, thrived, not despite the Church and owing little to the Church, but with its roots deep sunk in the Church's soil, and nourished by all that the Church offers as nourishment for the members of the body. And what does this mean but that the Spirit Who, within the Church, is the Spirit of truth, **is**, also within the Church, the Spirit of holiness ?

Finally, in the direct impact of the Church upon the world, both in the work of preaching the Gospel and in the testimony which the Church gives as to the things which belong to and create the world's best life, we see the presence and power of the Holy Spirit. It is the Spirit Who brings conviction to the world in respect of the fact and the deadliness of sin, the commanding claims of righteousness, and the reality of judgment. And for such action upon the world He uses not solely, yet in large measure, the Church. It is His presence, His inspiration, which kindles—and when the fire has sunk low, rekindles—the Church to walk worthy of her vocation. Some of the grandest aspects of the Church's task have the appearance of an adventurous voyage into uncharted seas. Each new age, as it comes, presents the Church with new problems and new responsibilities. Good, then, is it to remember the Apostle's word—Where the Spirit of the Lord is, there is liberty. The Church, in finding the true adjustment between herself and the movements and challenges of the age, has not to rely only on her mother-wit with the added wealth of her long experience. Not by might or power, not by worldly wisdom or craft of policy, is the contribution of the Church to the world to be made. The Church learns to serve the passing generations according to the will of God by the Spirit that dwells in her. For the life that she has is not given her for her private enjoyment, but that she may lead all men into the paths of peace and righteousness and of the knowledge of God. And nothing could more exalt in those who love her with the love of her own children the greatness and the

THE HOLY SPIRIT IN THE CHURCH

wonder of the Church than the continual memory of what her vocation is—the harvesting, through the Spirit, of the world, whose salvation drew the atoning Blood from Christ, and Christ from God.

All great and creative movements have their weaknesses. For into every movement enters on its human side something of the shortsightedness, of the failure sufficiently to expand our vision and to make it inclusive of all that it ought to include, which each one of us knows as a shortcoming and failure in the individual life. And because these congresses are not meetings for mutual congratulations, but, in part at least, for the clearer realization of the power of the Gospel for a fuller conversion of our country, it is not, I hope, out of place to say that while the Catholic revival in the Church of England has done a work of inestimable importance in its recovery of faith in the Holy Catholic Church, as one of the great articles of the Creed which lights up the meaning of Christianity and the promises and hopes of the Gospel, nevertheless, as it seems to me, the movement has not yet found itself, as it needs to find itself, does not speak with the power with which I would to God it did speak, in connection with the vast problems of social, industrial, and international life. That defect is to be remedied by deeper insight into the tremendous doctrine of the indwelling of the Holy Spirit in the Church. For it is, indeed, a tremendous doctrine, raising questions which, if pursued far enough, bring within their scope that one problem so manifold, so subtle, and yet so urgent, so critical for the life of both Church and world—the problem of the relationship which should exist between the

Church and the world. Easy solutions do not exist, but there can be no true solution at all, unless, first, we have learnt to bring together in the depth and breadth of our thoughts the Holy Catholic Church and the Holy Ghost Who dwells within her as her life. And as we learn so shall we give, give what men would hold with joy in their hearts, could their hearts but be opened to the vision—to the vision of a Catholic society, seeing by the light and glowing with the fire of a perpetual Pentecost, with its Lord's word as its charter to the nations : I am amongst you as he that serveth ; with its Lord's promise as its strength and stay : Ye shall receive power after that the Holy Ghost is come upon you.

www.ingramcontent.com/pod-product-compliance
Lightning Source LLC
Chambersburg PA
CBHW072131160426
43197CB00012B/2071